A Beginner's Guide to
Reading the Bible

Augsburg Beginner's Guides introduce readers to key subjects in the past and present of the Christian tradition. Beginner's Guides strive to be readable and yet reliable, simply written but not simplistic in their approach. Each book in the series includes the information that is needed for an overview of the subject and as a solid foundation for further study.

A Beginner's Guide to Reading the Bible
   by Craig R. Koester

A Beginner's Guide to the Books of the Bible
   by Diane L. Jacobson and Robert Kysar

A Beginner's Guide to Studying the Bible
   by Rolf E. Aaseng

A Beginner's Guide to

READING THE BIBLE

Craig R. Koester

Augsburg ▪ Minneapolis

A BEGINNER'S GUIDE TO READING THE BIBLE

The quotations in chapter 5 from the Gospel of Thomas are from the *Synopsis Quattuor Evangeliorum*, ed. Kurt Aland (Stuttgart: Deutsche Bibelstiftung, 1976), pp. 517, 530.

Photos: Keystone, 13; Religious News Service, 24, 57, 81; AP/Wide World Photos, 36; British Museum, 48, 78.

Maps: C. Kim Pickering

Cover design and illustration: Catherine Reishus McLaughlin

Library of Congress Cataloging-in-Publication Data

Koester, Craig R., 1953–
A beginner's guide to reading the Bible / Craig R. Koester.
p. cm.
Includes bibliographical references.
ISBN 0-8066-2570-8 (alk. paper)
1. Bible—Introductions. I. Title.
BS475.2.K66 1991
220.6'1—dc20 91-23447
CIP

The paper used in this publication meets the minimum requirements of American National Standard for Information Sciences—Permanence of Paper for Printed Library Materials, ANSI Z329.48-1984. ∞™

Manufactured in the U.S.A. AF 9-2570

04 11 12

Contents

Publisher's Preface

Many people are interested in the Bible, but hesitate to pick it up and begin reading because they may not know where to begin or may wonder whether they will be able to understand what they read. Even church members who have a strong desire to participate in formal Bible study classes may not do so, feeling that they first need a good orientation to the Bible.

A Beginner's Guide to Reading the Bible helps those who are not well acquainted with the Bible to overcome their fears and other obstacles that might hinder them from getting started. Even people who are already familiar with the Bible can gain much from this beginner's guide, since it offers a concise and clearly written review of the basics. It may also provide readers with some new information or new ways of looking at the Bible.

The Bible has been a source of spiritual strength, comfort, and guidance for countless people over the centuries. They have looked to it because of what it has to say about God, about human beings, and about our daily lives. In this book, author Craig Koester helps us enter into the world of the Bible and discover how it still speaks to us today.

1

Why Read
the Bible?

The word *Bible* comes from the Greek word *biblion* and simply means "book." In ordinary conversation, however, the word usually refers to one particular book, *the* Bible. People from the Arctic to southern Africa and from the Americas to Japan read the Bible. It has been translated into thousands of languages and dialects, and its stories and sayings have been told and retold until they have even been woven into the fabric of some cultures. If we ask people what the Bible is, however, the answers vary.

Car doors slam outside a small, white-frame church. A winter wind swirls the snow along the gravel driveway as several women hurry to the side door. Inside, the smell of coffee greets them. They hang their coats in the hall and walk to the folding chairs arranged around a table in the next room. The members of the group pull several well-thumbed Bibles and a short list of study questions from their bags, say a short prayer, and begin reading the passage for the day. They find that the Bible inspires faith and provides guidance for daily living.

A thousand miles away a crowd gathers by the steps of the United States capitol building. A chilly breeze ruffles the red, white, and blue bunting on the platform as the president-elect's motorcade arrives. Visiting dignitaries take their places and the chief justice of the Supreme Court steps to the podium. A Bible is produced. The president-elect places one hand on the Bible, raises the other hand, and vows to preserve, protect, and defend the Constitution of the United States. With that the inauguration itself is complete, and the speeches can begin. Here the Bible has served as a symbol of truth and authority.

Elsewhere, a student stands in line at a university bookstore. She rummages for her checkbook while balancing an armload of books for second semester classes: a biology textbook, a history of modern art, an introduction to psychology, and a paperback Bible for a course in world literature. As she makes out the check, she momentarily recalls the old family Bible on the living room shelf back home. It is a thick volume with Gothic lettering in a language her family can no longer understand; the names of her great-grandparents are inscribed inside the cover. She hands the check to the cashier, tucks the books into a canvas bag, and hurries off to class. For her, the Bible is a literary classic.

The Bible plays many roles in our society, not just one. The same book can be a source of inspiration and personal guidance, a source of truth and authority, a literary classic, and more. As you pick up the Bible you will have your own expectations about what it is. The rest of this chapter describes the various things you can gain by reading the Bible and what you may discover when you turn its pages.

The Bible and Faith

Some people turn to the Bible because they have faith. Others begin to read it because they are looking for faith. Both read the Bible for good reasons. The books of the Bible were written and preserved by communities of believers to nurture people in faith.

Many people would like their Bible reading to result in a dramatic growth in faith, and there are some famous incidents where this has happened. One of the most memorable stories is the conversion of Augustine, who became an influential leader and theologian in the early Christian church. When Augustine was a young man he experienced deep inner turmoil. He embarked on a spiritual quest, searching for meaning in his life. He joined a sectarian religious group known as the Manichees and read the works of Greek and Roman philosophers such as Cicero, Plato, and Aristotle. Still troubled by a nagging sense of guilt, he began attending Christian worship services and reading the Bible.

One day Augustine seemed to hear a child's voice repeating the words, "Take and read, take and read." Intrigued by what he heard, he opened the Scriptures and his eyes fell upon a verse that urged him to "put on the Lord Jesus Christ" (Romans 13:14). At that point the darkness of uncertainty vanished and his heart was flooded with the light of faith. Augustine confided this experience to his good friend Alypius, who had been enduring his own quiet spiritual struggle. Opening the Bible for himself, Alypius found that he, too, was strengthened in faith.

Augustine and Alypius experienced an immediate connection between Bible reading and faith. For most people, however, the value of Bible reading for faith becomes apparent only over a period of months or years. Faith does not come "automatically" when people read the Bible. Instead, the Holy Spirit uses the witness of the Scriptures to awaken and strengthen faith in God's own time. God alone can grant the gift of faith, but we can open the Scriptures and read them. The words enter into our minds and hearts like seeds settling into the earth, ready for the Spirit's gentle rain to awaken them to new life.

Sometimes the Bible nourishes faith through messages of comfort. For example, a child who hears the words, "The Lord is my shepherd," from Psalm 23:1, may find them gentle and assuring, like the words of a lullaby. Meanwhile, in the stark, white confines of a hospital ward, a cancer patient may find great strength in Psalm 23:4: "Even though I walk through the valley of the shadow of death, I will fear no evil; for thou art with me" (RSV). The Scriptures offer messages that can be grasped by the young, the old, and those in between. As life's seasons change, the Bible continues to offer its readers words of assurance, encouragement, refreshment, and hope. It is a book to grow with over a lifetime.

The Bible also strengthens faith by challenging and confronting its readers. For example, Jesus said, "You have heard that it was said to those of ancient times, 'You shall not murder'; and 'whoever murders shall be liable to judgment.' But I say to you that if you are angry with a brother or sister, you will be liable to judgment" (Matthew 5:21-23). Such harsh words have two purposes. First, the warnings help us curb the power of sin in our lives. Second, they confront us with the reality of our sin in order to turn us back to God. A physician will give a frank diagnosis of a disease to prepare a patient for treatment. In the same way, the Bible gives a candid judgment on human sin to help hold sin in check and prepare people for God's life-giving grace.

The Bible As an Authoritative Book

Dictionaries often define the Bible as the sacred book of the Christian church; something that is "sacred" or "holy" is something that is set apart for God's purposes. Christians themselves usually speak of the Bible as the Word of God and understand that it expresses God's will for people. Almost all Christian worship services include readings from the Bible, and most also have a sermon that helps bring the message of the Scriptures to bear on contemporary life. As the Word of God, the Bible is considered an authoritative book by Christians throughout the world. Most Protestant churches consider the Bible to be the primary authority in matters of Christian faith and life. The Roman Catholic and Orthodox churches hold that the Bible and church tradition together are authoritative for faith and morals.

Many Christians affirm that the Bible is authoritative because it was inspired by God. The word *inspired* is used in the Bible itself (2 Timothy 3:16) and is included in official statements of many Christian groups, including Baptist, Episcopal, Lutheran, Presbyterian, and Roman Catholic churches. Yet the Bible itself does not say *how* the inspiration took place and Christians have developed different positions on this issue. Some declare that each word in the Bible was communicated to the biblical authors by God. Others hold that the message was inspired but the actual words were not. Still others suggest that inspiration refers to the authors of the Bible, not to its words or message.

The differences arise because Christians agree that the Bible is the Word of God, but they also recognize that it is a human book. The Bible was written in languages spoken by ordinary human beings. At first, these languages were Hebrew, Aramaic, and Greek; later, the Bible was translated into other languages, making it accessible to people everywhere. The people who wrote down the material in the Bible had different writing styles. Some parts were written in elegant poetry, others in terse prose. The tone of writing spans from compassion to fury and from desperation to joy. Sometimes the biblical authors spoke in God's own name, saying, "Hear the word of the Lord!" Other passages include personal greetings from an author, comments about travel plans, and even a request to reserve a guest room.

Gutenburg Bibles. Johannes Gutenburg, the German inventor of the printing press, began printing Bibles (the Latin Vulgate) in 1456. Forty-eight of his Bibles are known to exist today in museums and private collections.

A useful way to think about the Bible's divine and human dimensions is to note that the Scriptures identify Jesus *himself* as the Word of God. The opening lines of John's Gospel say, "In the beginning was the Word, and the Word was with God, and the Word was God. . . . All things came into being through him. . . ." Later, the text says that "the Word became flesh and lived among us." It is in the life, death, and resurrection of Jesus Christ that God's love has been communicated most fully. The Bible, in turn, bears witness to what God has done in Christ.

13

Martin Luther, the sixteenth-century church reformer, urged people to open the Scriptures in order to find "that divine wisdom which God here lays before you in such simple guise as to quench all pride." He said, "Here you will find the swaddling cloths and the manger in which Christ lies, and to which the angel points the shepherds. Simple and lowly are these swaddling cloths, but dear is the treasure, Christ, who lies in them" (*Luther's Works*, vol. 35, Fortress Press, p. 236). Christians believe that the *words* of the Scriptures are authoritative because they are primary witnesses to the *Word*, Jesus Christ.

Christians who regard the Bible as authoritative for Christian faith and life generally recognize that the Bible demands careful interpretation. Often the need for interpretation becomes clear when people make startling or disturbing claims that they insist are supported by the Bible. For example, the Jehovah's Witnesses who take their message door-to-door will often hand out pamphlets filled with Bible passages describing what they believe will happen at the end of time. They may also challenge the views of other churches. When people are confronted by these teachings, they often sense a need to know more about what the Bible says and how biblical texts can be interpreted responsibly.

In a broader sense, reading the Bible engages people in ongoing reflection about what its message means for their lives. For example, when God created human beings, they were told to "have dominion over the fish of the sea and over the birds of the air and over every living thing that moves upon the earth" (Genesis 1:28). Each generation of Christians must ask what it means to be entrusted with such responsibility, and how that responsibility can be faithfully exercised. As Christians respond to these and other questions, the message of the Scriptures gives shape and direction to their lives.

Appreciating the Bible As Literature

The human dimension of the Bible noted earlier makes it possible to appreciate the Bible as a work of literature. Each day you probably read different kinds of literature, and the reading skills you have already developed will help you read the Bible. When you pick up a newspaper, for example, you recognize that it contains different kinds of material. You turn to the front page for information and scan the letters to the editor for readers' opinion. You understand that the advertisements are making a sales pitch and that the comics provide entertainment and social commentary.

Like a newspaper, the Bible contains many different kinds of material. You will find poetry, history, prophecy, and parable as you explore its pages. When you read the sentence, "In the fourteenth year of King Hezekiah, King Sennacherib of Assyria came up against all the fortified cities of Judah and captured them" (2 Kings 18:13), you assume you are reading history. When you read, "Let the floods clap their hands; let the hills sing together for joy" (Psalm 98:8), you quickly realize that you are reading poetry that uses figurative language. Both history and poetry can convey truth, but they do so in quite different ways. The skills you have developed by reading other kinds of writing will help you distinguish between the different sorts of material found in the Bible and help you approach each type of writing in an appropriate way.

A student who purchases a Bible for a course in world literature will be asked to read the Bible as he or she would read other classic writings. An instructor may focus on plot development in some portion of the Bible, analyze the role of the narrator, or explore the ways characters are portrayed. The class may compare and contrast the Bible with ancient poetry by Virgil or a modern novel by James Joyce. Such comparisons are possible because literary forms such as poetry and narrative are not unique to the Bible, but are also used in other sorts of writing.

Readers are attracted by the varying moods and intriguing plots within the Bible. These enhance its value for readers, including those who regard the Bible as authoritative Scripture. The mood of the Bible ranges from exuberant joy to deep sorrow. Its dramatic narratives feature people who labored as fishermen and home-makers, soldiers and politicians. In some passages the power and presence of God are readily apparent. In other places God is rarely mentioned, as kings maneuver for power and sages share their wisdom; men and women fall in love, marry, and raise families; siblings quarrel and become reconciled.

The Bible tells the story of God and the stories of human beings. It is a book with many dimensions. God's Spirit works through the witness of the Scriptures to awaken and strengthen faith. Christian churches throughout the world recognize the Bible's authority for Christian life and teaching, and as people reflect on its message, it can give shape and direction to their lives. The Bible's poetry and prose, its stories and songs also make it a varied and engaging work of literature. Your appreciation of the Bible will grow as you keep its many roles in view. In the following chapters we will explore different facets of the Bible, including its contents, origins, interpretation, and translation, to help you discover the richness of the biblical texts themselves.

2

What Is in
the Bible?

The Bibles we use today are single volumes with many pages, and we often think of the Bible as a single book. But to open the Bible is actually to enter a great library containing many books that were written at different times and places by different people. The "biblical library" used by Protestants contains sixty-six individual books, which are listed in the table of contents in the front of a modern Bible (see the chart on p. 19). The Roman Catholic and Orthodox churches have additional books in their Bibles, and the reasons for this will be discussed in chapter 5.

Over the centuries the scribes who copied and preserved the biblical library developed a reference system to help readers locate specific items in the collection. Each book of the Bible is divided into chapters of varying length, which are marked by a large number on the pages of the text. Each chapter, in turn, is divided into smaller units called "verses," which are usually one or two sentences long, and are identified by the small numbers within each chapter. References to specific biblical texts first give the name of the book, then the chapter number, followed by a colon and the verse number. For example, Genesis 1:3 refers to Genesis, the first book of the Bible, chapter one, verse three, which begins, "Then God said, 'Let there be light.' "

Like a modern library that is divided into subject areas, the Bible is divided into different sections. One large section of the biblical library is called the Old Testament and the other is the New Testament. A "testament" is a written expression of someone's will, and the Old and New Testaments express the will of God for people. The first part of the Bible, or "Old Testament," was written down and preserved over many centuries prior to the coming of Christ. It bears witness to the promises God made to the people of Israel. For Jewish people, what Christians refer to as the Old Testament is the entire Bible. Christian Bibles also include the New Testament, which was written between A.D. 50 and A.D. 110, and bears witness to the saving work of Jesus Christ.

For many years the books of the Old Testament were grouped into three categories: the Law, the Prophets, and the Writings. A form of this arrangement was in use when the New Testament was written (Luke 24:44) and is still used by Jewish people today. Christian Bibles have arranged the material somewhat differently, in four main categories: the Law, the Historical books, Wisdom materials, and the Prophets. The New Testament begins with the four Gospels, which tell the story of Jesus; next comes the book of Acts, which is a history of the early church; finally there is a series of letters written by leaders of the early church.

People who use a library naturally look for the books that will be most interesting to them. Those who read the Bible will likewise want to turn first to the biblical books that seem most pertinent. A brief tour through the various sections of the biblical library will reveal the wealth of material contained within them. For further information, see *A Beginner's Guide to the Books of the Bible,* which provides introductions to each of the thirty-nine books of the Old Testament and twenty-seven books of the New Testament (see "For Further Reading" on p. 97).

The Law, or Pentateuch

The first five books of the Bible—Genesis, Exodus, Leviticus, Numbers, and Deuteronomy—are often called "the Law," but they actually contain a great deal more than just legal materials. In addition to the statues and ordinances of Israel,* these books

---

*The name *Israel* can mean several different things: one of the Old Testament patriarchs (also known as Jacob); God's chosen people; the land or country that God promised to give to the people of Israel; and a kingdom established in the northern part of that country.

How the Books [of the Bib]le Are Organized

The Bible is divided into two [Test]aments." The Old Testament contains four major sections that include 39 individual books. The New Testament is divided into three sections that include 27 books.

The Old Testament	The New Testament
The Pentateuch Genesis Exodus Leviticus Numbers Deuteronomy	*The Gospels* Matthew Mark Luke John
History Joshua Judges Ruth 1 and 2 Samuel 1 and 2 Kings 1 and 2 Chronicles Ezra Nehemiah Esther	*History* Acts of the Apostles *The Letters* Romans 1 and 2 Corinthians Galatians Ephesians Philippians Colossians 1 and 2 Thessalonians 1 and 2 Timothy
Wisdom Job Psalms Proverbs Ecclesiastes Song of Solomon	Titus Philemon Hebrews James 1 and 2 Peter 1, 2, and 3 John Jude Revelation
Prophets Isaiah Jeremiah Lamentations Ezekiel Daniel Hosea Joel Amos Obadiah Jonah Micah Nahum Habakkuk Zephaniah Haggai Zechariah Malachi	

include poems, songs, and epic narratives about the people of God. More useful titles for this section are the Hebrew word *Torah,* which means "instruction," and the Greek term *Pentateuch,* which means "the five (*penta*) books." Unlike modern novels, which are usually written from start to finish by a single author, the books of the Pentateuch are collections of materials written down by different people at different times.

The book of Genesis begins with two accounts of the world's creation. The majestic poetry of the first account (Genesis 1:1— 2:4) tells how God spoke and on six successive days the earth and heaven and all living things came into being. The epic culminates with the creation of men and women on the sixth day and God resting on the seventh day. The grand harmony of the creative process is accented by the refrain "And God saw that it was good." The second story (Genesis 2:4-24) goes back to the beginning again, to the time before there were any plants or people, to tell how God created a man, then the lush foliage of a garden, the animals, and finally a woman. Together, these two stories bear witness in different ways to God's work as creator and the role of human beings as caretakers of creation.

The remainder of Genesis tells of the world's fall into sin and recounts the stories of the people who were chosen to carry out God's redemptive purposes. The text does not trace the rise and fall of empires, but focuses on people who would ordinarily be overlooked by the history books. For example, Abraham was a herdsman whom God chose to become the father of a great nation that would bring a blessing to all the peoples of the earth (Genesis 12:2-3). Abraham and his wife Sarah grew old and soon laughed at the idea that they could have children. In the end God must have chuckled, however, because Sarah bore a son named Isaac, meaning "he laughs." Their descendants grew in number but were plagued by family rivalries and intrigues. Throughout much of the story God remained in the background, but as their jealousies gave way to reconciliation, it became clear that God's life-giving purposes were quietly being carried out all along (Genesis 50:20).

The book of Exodus recounts the liberation of God's people from slavery in Egypt. God chose a man named Moses to deliver the people. Moses stammered his objections, but God managed

to persuade him to demar   e king of Egypt release the
people. The king repeatec   d. Then, after suffering ten
plagues from God, he relentea momentarily, only to change his
mind again. Trapped between the pursuing Egyptian army and
the sea, the people escaped as God parted the waters before them.
The Egyptian army gave chase, but the waters closed over their
chariots and the people of God were free (Exodus 14). When they
arrived at Mt. Sinai they were given the Ten Commandments
(Exodus 20:1-17), which begin by proclaiming what God has
done: "I am the Lord your God, who brought you out of the land
of Egypt, out of the house of slavery." The commandments first
state that people are to honor the God who has saved them. They
should do this by refusing to worship any other deities or abuse
God's name, and by observing the Sabbath as a day of rest. The
commandments also deal with ways people should relate to one
other, by showing respect for parents and by refusing to murder,
engage in adultery, steal, commit perjury, or to covet what belongs
to another.

The more extensive collections of laws contained in the remainder of Exodus, Leviticus, Numbers, and Deuteronomy provide additional directions for the ways the people of Israel were
to relate to God. Some of the ordinances provided for sacrifices,
through which people received forgiveness of their sins. There
were also provisions for making a movable sanctuary, a tent in
which God promised to meet with the people as they journeyed
toward the promised land. Other regulations distinguished clean
from unclean foods and established procedures for purifying one's
body and home.

Many of the laws also deal with ways people should relate to
one another. Some sections establish procedures to deal justly
with criminal offenses, such as murder and theft. Other passages
discuss who is responsible for damages when someone is injured
because of negligence. Still other parts deal with matters of sexual
conduct, prohibiting incest and other forms of sexual activity that
are destructive to individual and community alike. Taken together, the statutes found in the Pentateuch make it clear that
Israel's special relationship with God was intended to affect all
aspects of the people's life.

Historical Writings

The books of Joshua through Esther were composed at different times and places, but have been arranged in a sequence that recounts the history of the people of Israel over a period of several centuries. Like the narrative portions of the Pentateuch, these books focus on God's chosen people; they are not comprehensive history textbooks. The book of Joshua shows God's faithfulness to Israel by telling how God brought the people into possession of the promised land. The book of Judges recounts how Israel repeatedly broke faith with God by worshiping other deities and how the people were oppressed by other nations until God delivered them. The books of Samuel and Kings chronicle the rise and fall of the kings of Israel. They tell the tragic story of Saul, recall the golden era of David and Solomon, and trace the repeated disloyalty toward God among many of their successors, which finally led to the destruction of the kingdom.

As you read these histories you will find that they contain more than simple narratives. A jubilant song celebrates the victory of the prophetess Deborah over the kings of Canaan (Judges 5). A fable is told concerning a man named Abimelech who tried to make himself a king over Israel; the moral is that Abimelech had no more right to rule Israel than a bramble should be elevated above an olive tree (Judges 9:7-15). A prophet named Nathan told King David a parable about a rich man who arrogantly took a lamb from a poor man. When David cried out that the rich man had acted unjustly, Nathan retorted that the king himself was that rich man who had wrongly taken another man's wife (2 Samuel 12:1-15). The rich tapestry of narrative, song, fable, and parable provides an elegant testimony to the ways of God with his people.

Wisdom Books

The books of Job, Psalms, Proverbs, Ecclesiastes, and Song of Solomon are written in poetic style. Many Bibles print these texts line by line, instead of in paragraph form, to highlight their poetic character. These writings can be loosely grouped together as books of "wisdom." Wisdom literature gives counsel on the living of life and attempts to make sense of the problems people face.

The book of Job is a drama that probes the mystery of human suffering, asking why bad things happen to good people. Job was a just and devout man who tragically lost his property, his children, and his health. Several friends advised him that such suffering had to be God's just punishment for some sort of wrongdoing, but Job rejected their explanation, demanding to know how such excessive suffering could possibly be seen as fair punishment. Finally God himself spoke to Job out of a whirlwind, asking him to look at the creation and observe how God cared for all living things in ways that were beyond Job's understanding. In the end the book does not explain suffering, but shows how people can continue to live, despite their suffering, through faith in God.

The book of Psalms is the Bible's hymnal. It is a collection of one hundred and fifty songs and poems, many of which were used in Israel's worship. The vivid imagery and graceful style of the Psalms have inspired worshipers for generations, and many hymns used in churches today continue to use the ancient lyrics in new ways. Some psalms come out of the wisdom tradition, comparing a godly person to a tree bearing rich fruit, in contrast to the wicked who are like chaff driven away by the wind (Psalm 1). Other psalms are exuberant hymns, shouting "Make a joyful noise to the LORD, all the earth. Worship the LORD with gladness; come into his presence with singing" (Psalm 100:1-2). Still other psalms pour out human sorrow to God, crying "Out of the depths I cry to you, O LORD. Lord, hear my voice!" (Psalm 130:1-2). These hymns span the full range of human life and emotion, putting into words the joys and sorrows of the people of God.

The book of Proverbs is a collection of maxims that counsel people to live prudent and godly lives. The text advises readers that the ways of wisdom bring happiness and peace, while the paths of folly lead to trouble. The author of Ecclesiastes, however, offers a more pessimistic view of life. The author laments that "in much wisdom is much vexation, and those who increase knowledge increase sorrow" (Ecclesiastes 1:18), for there is no real gain, but life is simply an empty "chasing after wind." The Song of Solomon is a collection of intimate poems extolling the grandeur of love between a man and a woman. When viewed together, (the books in the wisdom section of the biblical library deal with human life and experience in all its diversity.)

Prophetic Books

The remaining books of the Old Testament preserve the testimonies of Israel's prophets. The longest books, known as the "major prophets," are Isaiah, Jeremiah, and Ezekiel. These are followed by the book of Daniel, and the twelve shorter books that are called the "minor prophets," including Hosea through Malachi. The prophecies contained in these books do not simply predict the future. Many passages comment on the society in which the prophets lived. They condemn idolatry and injustice, and advocate faithfulness toward God and justice for those in need.

This scroll of Isaiah is nearly 24 feet long and is made up of 17 sheets of parchment sewn together.

The passages that do speak of the future sometimes warn of the judgments soon coming upon Israel, while other texts envision a time when God creates "new heavens and a new earth" (Isaiah 65:17). As a group, these books present powerful words of judgment and hope that have spoken to people across the centuries.

Many parts of these writings are composed in a poetic style, like that found in the wisdom writings. The book of Isaiah begins by lamenting that "the ox knows its owner, and the donkey its master's crib; but Israel does not know, my people do not understand" (Isaiah 1:3). Other portions recount visions received by the prophets. One of the most vivid experiences was that of Isaiah, who saw the Lord sitting upon his throne, attended by fiery angels called "seraphim." One of these touched the lips of the prophet with a burning coal to prepare him to speak in the name of God (Isaiah 6).

Some of the books provide glimpses into the lives of the prophets. Jeremiah 19 and 20, for example, tell how Jeremiah shattered an earthenware jug in front of the leaders of the people as a sign of the destruction coming upon Israel. He was arrested and subjected to public ridicule by being placed in stocks, but confessed that God's word was like a burning fire within his bones and he could not keep silent about it. Hosea was called upon to marry a prostitute as a sign of God's love for Israel, who had prostituted herself by worshiping other gods (Hosea 1:2). Amos was a herdsman and a field hand who pruned sycamore trees until God called him as a prophet to Israel. By means of their words and lives the prophets bore witness to God's will for his people, and their books conclude the Old Testament section of the library.

The Gospels and Acts

The New Testament begins with four accounts of the life of Jesus called "Gospels,"—Matthew, Mark, Luke, and John. The Greek word for gospel is *evangelion* (the root of our words "evangelist" and "evangelism"), which simply means "good news." The term was often used to describe a messenger racing down a path, heralding the good news of a victory in a battle. The first four books of the New Testament proclaim the good news or "gospel" of God's victory over the powers of sin and death by telling the story of Jesus' life, death, and resurrection. Those who wrote the four New Testament Gospels were impassioned messengers who told the story so "that you may believe that Jesus is the Christ, the Son of God, and that believing you may have life in his name" (John 20:31 RSV).

Although the four Gospels tell the same story, each portrays Jesus in its own distinctive way. Matthew depicts Jesus as the teacher of Israel by tracing his ancestry back into Israel's history (Matthew 1), including the lengthy summary of his teaching often called "the Sermon on the Mount" (Matthew 5–7), and concluding with Jesus' commission to make disciples of all nations, "teaching them to obey everything that I have commanded you" (Matthew 28:20). Mark portrays Jesus more as the suffering Messiah, who repeatedly battled the forces of evil, was misunderstood by his own disciples, and whose true identity was revealed only through his grim death by crucifixion. Luke presents Jesus as the royal Savior, whose story begins with a humble birth in Bethlehem, the city where king David once lived, and ends with Jesus' ascension to the right hand of God in heaven. John's Gospel introduces Jesus as the divine Son of God (John 1:1-18), who uniquely revealed God's glory and love through his works, teachings, death, and resurrection.

The fifth book of the New Testament is the book of Acts, which is a history of the early church written by the author of Luke's Gospel. Like the historical writings in the Old Testament, the book of Acts recounts events that show the purposes of God. The text describes how Jesus' followers were empowered by the Holy Spirit to spread the gospel message throughout much of the Roman Empire, despite opposition from many of Israel's leaders.

The Letters

The rest of the New Testament consists of letters or "epistles" written by early Christian leaders to members of Christian congregations. Thirteen of these are attributed to the apostle Paul and are named for the cities or individuals to whom the letters were sent (Romans through Philemon; see Map 5). The other letters are named for their authors. Many of the letters follow a similar format, beginning with a greeting from the author to the intended recipients and words of thanksgiving. The body of the letter then discusses matters of concern and concludes with exhortations and greetings.

The contents of these letters address a broad spectrum of issues confronting Christian people. Often they begin with a proclamation of the gospel, the good news of God's victory over the powers of sin and death. Then the letters go on to investigate how the good news informs specific situations confronting Christians, such as bickering within a congregation (1 Corinthians 3), marriage, divorce, and singleness (1 Corinthians 7), or the death of loved ones (1 Thessalonians 4:13-18). The tone of the letters ranges from compassion and joy to anger and exasperation as the authors seek to address the real concerns of Christian people.

The last book of the Bible is the book of Revelation. Although it is sometimes treated as a unique piece of writing, it too is a letter. Like the letters of Paul, the book of Revelation begins with greetings from the author to the seven churches that were to receive it (Revelation 1:4-5). The next two chapters speak in some detail of the issues confronting each congregation (Revelation 2–3). The author of the book wrote down the visions contained in chapters 4 through 22 in order to address the needs of these congregations. The meaning of the details in the visions sometimes remains unclear, but like the letters of Paul, the book of Revelation presents a message of warning and hope that was intended to strengthen the faith of the Christians to whom it was addressed.

Taken together, the books in the biblical library form a rich collection containing history, poetry, songs, letters, prophecies, sermons, and parables. Yet the many and varied voices within the Scriptures join in a single chorus, bearing witness to the creative, saving, and sustaining work of God.

3

How Was the Old Testament Formed?

Those who enter the world of the Old Testament find themselves journeying thousands of years back in time to a world that can seem strange to modern eyes. The people who inhabit the pages of Scripture knew nothing of computers, nuclear power, or space travel, but trudged slowly across the plains of history on foot, or perhaps by camel or chariot. Many of the figures in the Old Testament lived in tribal societies in which men sometimes had two or more wives and wealth was measured by the size of one's flocks and herds. A man could woo his beloved by telling her that her "hair is like a flock of goats" and her "teeth are like a flock of shorn ewes" (Song of Solomon 4:1-2), words that sound odd to the ears of most readers today.

A sketch of the biblical landscape and the way in which the Old Testament took shape can help modern readers feel more at home with these ancient texts. Those who step into the world of the Bible will see how the Scriptures have addressed issues confronting the people of God in generation after generation. By listening carefully to the ways the biblical texts spoke in ancient times, we can better understand how they can continue to speak in our time.

Israel's Origins

The story of Israel's origins emerges only gradually from the mists of history. There is much that is unknown about Israel's earliest ancestors. According to the book of Genesis, the story began with Abraham and Sarah between about 2000 and 1700 B.C. (see the chart on pp. 32-33). They first lived at the far eastern end of the Old Testament world, not far from the Persian Gulf (see Map 1). Gradually they migrated westward through the fertile plains watered by the Tigris and Euphrates rivers in what is now Iraq and Syria. According to Genesis 12, God called Abraham to leave this area and go to the land that God would show him. God also promised that Abraham would be blessed, that his descendants would become a great nation, and that through him all the nations of the earth would be blessed. Abraham responded to God's call and finally settled in the land of Canaan, a narrow band of land known today as Palestine or Israel. The languages of the region were Semitic dialects, including Hebrew and Aramaic, the languages in which the Old Testament was written.

Abraham's family pastured their flocks and herds in the hill country and semi-arid plains of Canaan, worshiping God at sacred sites near their encampments. Various crises periodically forced them to leave the country. Droughts sometimes drove them into Egypt. Abraham sent a servant to the old country to bring back a wife for his son Isaac so that he would not marry a Canaanite. Isaac's son Jacob, in turn, fled eastward to escape the rage of his brother, find a wife, and make his fortune before returning to Canaan. Jacob himself (whose name was changed by God to "Israel") had twelve sons, but because of family rivalry, one of them, named Joseph, was sold as a slave and taken to Egypt. There he managed to become a high-ranking official, and when famine drove the rest of the family into Egypt, the brothers became reconciled and settled there permanently.

Their descendants, who were then called Hebrews or "children of Israel," continued to live in Egypt for roughly four centuries, from about 1700 to 1275 B.C. During that time they were enslaved by the Egyptians and forced to make bricks and mortar under the lash of the king's overseers. A Hebrew named Moses saw an Egyptian beating one of his kinsmen. Moses killed the Egyptian and fled to the desert regions east of Egypt. There he was called by God to return to Egypt and deliver his people from slavery. Israel's deliverance from Egypt is commonly known as the "Exodus" and is one of the pivotal events in the Old Testament (see Map 1). The biblical account says that Moses returned to Egypt and told the king that the Hebrew people must be freed. When the king of Egypt refused, the Egyptians were afflicted with various plagues. The water of the Nile River became foul, frogs and insects multiplied, and diseases, hail, and darkness made life miserable for the Egyptians. Finally, after the firstborn children and animals of each Egyptian household suddenly died, the Egyptians momentarily relented and the people of Israel fled eastward by night. The Egyptians pursued them, but the Israelites escaped recapture by miraculously crossing a sea while the Egyptian chariots were swept away by the water.

The people of Israel began their new life of freedom by remaining in the desert regions east of Egypt for about forty years, from approximately 1275 to 1235 B.C. The central event of this period was establishing a covenant relationship between God and Israel at Mt. Sinai. The covenant reminded the people that it was God who had brought them "out of the land of Egypt, out of the house of slavery" (Exodus 20:2), and called upon them to honor God alone and reject the deities of other nations. The primary provisions of this covenant, known as the Ten Commandments, became Israel's charter as a nation.

After departing from Mt. Sinai, the people gradually moved north and east into what is now the kingdom of Jordan. The generation that escaped out of Egypt, including Moses himself, died out as the people of Israel approached the Jordan River and prepared to enter the land of Canaan once again.

The details of Israel's entry into the land are unclear, but the biblical account suggests that conquest began about 1235 B.C. under the leadership of Joshua. Military victories at various places in Canaan apparently helped Israel gain possession of part of the land, but the westward movement of the Israelites was halted by the Philistines, who held sizable portions of the country. For generations the twelve tribes of Israel led a precarious existence in Canaan, often subjugated by neighboring peoples until a leader arose to liberate them. One of these leaders or "judges" was Deborah, a prophetess who led the people to a stunning victory over the Canaanites. During the rout the Canaanite general sought shelter in a tent, where another woman drove a tent peg through his head while he was sleeping. Another judge was the strong

31

Chronology of the Old Testament

Based on information found in the Bible and in other ancient sources, it is possible to reconstruct a general chronology of Old Testament events and approximate dates for the completion of biblical books. Dates prior to the time of the United Monarchy are often uncertain, and there is disagreement about the dating of certain Old Testament books.

	Approximate Dates	People and Events	A Sample of Old Testament Books
1. Ancestral Period	2000–1700 B.C.	Abraham, Sarah and their descendants; Migration to Canaan	Stories circulate orally
2. Sojourn in Egypt	1700–1275 B.C.	Migration to Egypt; Period of slavery	
3. Exodus and Wilderness Wanderings	1275–1235 B.C.	Moses, giving of Ten Commandments	
4. Period of Conquest	1235–1200 B.C.	Joshua	
5. Period of the Judges	1200–1050 B.C.	Deborah, Gideon, Samson, Samuel	
6. United Monarchy	1050–922 B.C.	Saul, David, Solomon; Construction of original Temple	Parts of the Pentateuch compiled in written form
7. Divided Monarchy			
A. The Northern Kingdom (Israel)	922–721 B.C.	Kings: Jereboam I, Ahab and others; Prophets: Elijah, Elisha, Hosea, Amos; Kingdom conquered by Assyria	More of the Pentateuch written down; Hosea, Amos
B. The Southern Kingdom (Judah)	922–586 B.C.	Kings: Rehoboam, Hezekiah and others; Prophets: Isaiah, Micah, Jeremiah; Kingdom conquered by Babylonia	Isaiah 1–39, Micah, Jeremiah, Deuteronomy, many Psalms

8. Period of the Exile	586–538 B.C.	Ezekiel	Ezekiel, remainder of Pentateuch, Isaiah 40–66, Samuel and Kings completed, some Psalms
9. Persian Period	538–330 B.C.	Ezra, Nehemiah; Return to Jerusalem; Temple is rebuilt	Ezra, Nehemiah, Chronicles, Haggai, Zechariah, Jonah
10. Hellenistic Period	330–165 B.C.	Palestine conquered by Alexander the Great	Ecclesiastes
11. Maccabean Period	165–63 B.C.	Hasmonean family or "Maccabees" establish Israel as independent kingdom; Comes under Roman control in 63 B.C.	Daniel

man Samson, who repeatedly fraternized with Philistine women and then avenged himself against Philistine villages when the relationships turned sour. The stories of Israel's heroes and ancestors were passed along orally from generation to generation, but were not yet put into writing (see the chart on p. 32).

Israel under the Kings

The continued threat of being dominated by other nations finally led the people of Israel to clamor for a king who could lead them. Samuel, the last of the judges, designated a man named Saul as Israel's first king. Saul was a tall and handsome man who was sometimes swept up into spiritual ecstasy. Soon after becoming king, Saul demonstrated his ability by leading the Israelite army to victory. But later Saul was plagued by sharp mood swings and became jealous of the popularity enjoyed by David, a promising young man from Bethlehem who was a member of his court. David fled for his life and lived as the leader of an outlaw band at the periphery of the country until Saul was wounded in battle and committed suicide.

David became king about 1000 B.C. and ushered in Israel's golden age. He helped to unify Israel by capturing the city of Jerusalem, which was in the middle of the country, and making it his capital. Under David's leadership a series of successful military campaigns secured Israel's borders against the neighboring peoples. One of David's own sons tried to seize his throne, driving him into temporary exile, but David managed to regain power. Another son named Solomon was designated as David's successor.

Solomon's outstanding achievement was the construction of a temple in Jerusalem, which became the religious as well as the political center of the country. International commerce was expanded, the arts flourished, and an opulent palace was built for the king. To carry out his building projects, Solomon enslaved some of the non-Israelite peoples within his realm, and to secure his political position, he entered into several foreign alliances. He sealed these pacts by marrying women from the various allied peoples, and he permitted shrines to foreign deities in Jerusalem, even though worship of other gods had traditionally been condemned in Israel.

It was during this period that portions of the Old Testament began to be written down (see the chart on p. 32). The rise of a powerful monarchy in Israel posed new questions about Israel's relationship to the nations. Some of the old stories about Israel's ancestors that had been handed on orally for generations were written down in a way that helped provide a perspective on the new situation. For example, the stories of Adam and Eve (Genesis 2–3) and the Tower of Babel (Genesis 11:1-9) warned the prosperous nation about the dangers of self-aggrandizement. The story of Abraham's call (Genesis 12:1-3) reminded people that Israel had become a great nation in fulfillment of God's promise and that God had chosen them to be a blessing to all the families of the earth.

The rise of the monarchy and establishment of the temple also provided the context in which many of the psalms were written. King David was known for his love of music, and some of the psalms have been attributed to him, but most of the psalms were composed over a period of several centuries by unknown authors connected with the temple and royal house. Some of the psalms

34

were used amid the pageantry of worship in the temple. Psalm 134:1-2 exhorts worshipers to "Come, bless the Lord, all you servants of the Lord, who stand by night in the house of the Lord! Lift up your hands to the holy place, and bless the Lord!" Other psalms honored the king. One courtier wrote, "My heart overflows with a goodly theme; I address my verses to the king. . . . You are the most handsome of men; grace is poured upon your lips" (Psalm 45:1-2).

After Solomon died, his son Rehoboam ruled harshly and the kingdom split in two in 922 B.C. (see Map 3). The northern part was still called Israel, the southern part was called Judah, and relations between the two kingdoms shifted between uneasy co-existence and open hostility. The northern kingdom entered into close relations with the nations to the north, and the worship of the god Baal and goddess Astarte became common. The prophet Elijah protested the worship of these deities and challenged the priests of Baal to demonstrate the power of their gods by calling down fire from heaven. When they were unable to do so, Elijah prayed to the God of Israel, fire fell from heaven, and Elijah's followers slaughtered the prophets of Baal (1 Kings 18:17-40). In the eighth century B.C., the prophets Amos and Hosea joined the protest against the idolatrous and unjust practices of the northern kingdom. Finally, in 721 B.C., the army of Assyria, a powerful nation to the northeast, conquered the northern kingdom of Israel and exiled its leaders (see Map 2).

Meanwhile the southern kingdom of Judah also struggled with issues of idolatry and injustice. The oppressive practices of Judah's leaders were denounced by prophets such as Micah, who came from a village in the foothills, and Isaiah, a resident of Jerusalem. Some reforms were undertaken by King Hezekiah in the late eighth century B.C., but his successors reverted to patterns of corruption. The prophet Jeremiah, who came from a priestly family, railed against Israel's attraction to foreign cults, some of which included child sacrifice. He warned that if Judah did not repent, it would be devastated like the northern kingdom had been.

The words of the prophets sometimes were written down and preserved by their followers. Isaiah had a group of disciples who preserved his teachings (Isaiah 8:16), and Jeremiah dictated his

Tombstone of King Uzziah, 785–734 B.C. The Aramaic inscription reads, "To this place were brought the bones of Uzziah, King of Judah. Do not open."

pronouncements to a scribe named Baruch (Jeremiah 36:4). As you read the books of the prophets, you will find messages that were originally delivered at different times and places now placed side by side in the text. Some have a formal introduction, like "An oracle concerning Moab" (Isaiah 15:1), but the beginnings and endings of other oracles can only be discerned by changes in the tone or contents. Some Bibles insert headings in the text or provide footnotes to help readers understand these passages.

Reforms were undertaken in the late seventh century B.C., during the reign of Josiah; the book of Deuteronomy probably stems from this period. It declares, "Hear, O Israel: The Lord is our God, the Lord alone. You shall love the Lord your God with all your heart, and with all your soul, and with all your might" (Deuteronomy 6:4). The book also calls for worship at one central sanctuary, rather than at various local shrines which all too readily became havens for pagan worship. A first edition of Joshua, Judges, Samuel, and Kings also may have come from this period, recounting the calamities that befell the people when they became faithless. In the end, however, Judah was conquered by the Babylonians in 586 B.C., and Judah's leading citizens were exiled to Babylonia far to the northeast (see Map 2).

Exile and Return

The Babylonian exile was one of the great crises in Israel's history. People questioned how God could permit the brutal destruction of Jerusalem and the loss of Israel's homeland. Traditions were written down that addressed the concerns of people living in this period (see the chart on p. 33). The poetic account of the creation (Genesis 1) reminded people that all the earth belonged to God. The story of the portable tent sanctuary that Israel used while wandering in the desert after the exodus from Egypt (Exodus 25–40) assured them that God could be worshiped in many places, not just in Jerusalem. An anonymous prophet whose work is preserved in Isaiah 40–55 assured the people that the God who once made a way for Israel through the sea during the Exodus would deliver them once again. The prophet Ezekiel told the exiles that even though Israel seemed as lifeless as a field of dry bones, God would revitalize the people and take them home again (Ezekiel 37:1-14). The books of Joshua, Judges, Samuel, and Kings were also expanded, emphasizing that the northern and southern kingdoms had fallen because of their own religious apostasy, not because God was unfaithful.

A turning point came when Cyrus, king of Persia, conquered Babylonia. In 538 B.C., Cyrus declared that the exiles, now known as Judeans or Jews, could return to their country. Some of the exiles chose to remain in Babylonia, but others returned and began the slow task of reconstruction. Urged on by prophets such as Haggai and Zechariah, whose writings appear in the Old Testament, the people eventually established a new temple and rebuilt Jerusalem. The scribes Ezra and Nehemiah called for renewed commitment to the laws and traditions of Israel that were being assembled into the form in which we now have them in the Pentateuch (Genesis, Exodus, Leviticus, Numbers, and Deuteronomy). Together, the temple and the law became the two institutions that gave the people their distinct identity while living under Persian domination.

By the fifth century B.C. the Pentateuch had probably assumed its final shape. The process had taken many centuries. Stories and statutes circulated orally for generations before being written down, then these shorter documents were combined into written collections. This long process left a number of repetitions and inconsistencies in the text. For example, the book of Genesis tells the story of a great flood that engulfed the world. Before sending the torrential rains, God told Noah to build a boat and bring into it two of every kind of living thing, which Noah did (Genesis 6:19-22). But in the next paragraph God commanded Noah to bring *seven* pairs of every species into the boat, which Noah also did (Genesis 7:1-5). Apparently there were once two separate versions of this story, one in which Noah saved one pair of each species and one in which Noah saved seven pairs. Instead of choosing one version over the other, both versions were combined into a single narrative. Similar repetitions occur in other narratives as well. The people who collected and preserved these stories apparently were not disturbed by the inconsistencies, but assumed that the basic message was clear.

The other literature composed and collected during this period reflects the importance of the law and the temple for Israel's life. Psalm 119, the longest psalm in the Bible, extols the glories of God's law, testimonies, ordinances, and statutes. When the Psalms were arranged in a single collection, they were introduced by a psalm advising readers that those who delight in the law of the Lord and meditate upon it day and night are blessed (Psalm 1:2). The books of Chronicles retell some of the stories found in Samuel and Kings, with extensive attention given to the temple and its administration.

A significant change in the cultural climate of the Old Testament world began when Alexander the Great swept down from Macedonia and Greece to conquer Palestine in 330 B.C. He also conquered most of the known world. Until this time the prevailing cultural winds had come from the east, from the kingdoms of Assyria, Babylonia, and Persia. Now the winds shifted and began coming from the west. Alexander envisioned a grand world city in which people would not belong primarily to a given tribe or local community, but to the Greek Empire. One would become a citizen of this world community by learning the Greek language and Greek culture and by adopting Greek ways. The citizens of this new world community would tolerate one another's religious beliefs in the conviction that Jupiter, Zeus, and Baal, or Venus, Aphrodite, and Astarte were simply the same gods and goddesses worshiped under different names. Greek cities with their theaters, gymnasiums, and stadiums were established to administer the empire and spread Greek culture. After Alexander's death, his empire was divided among his successors, but the vision of one world city persisted.

Jews at this time were living in many different parts of the empire. Many of them now spoke Greek, and parts of the Old Testament were translated from Hebrew into Greek so that they could read it. But the new vision of one world city differed significantly from the conviction that Israel was God's chosen people. Some of the Jewish people liked the new vision and began adopting Greek customs, but others rebelled and insisted that to do so would be to commit apostasy. The governor of that region tried to suppress the revolt by forbidding observance of Israel's law and by turning the Jerusalem temple into a shrine that he dedicated to Zeus in 167 B.C. This crisis is reflected in the visions of the book of Daniel, which lament the desecration of the temple and anticipate the coming of divine judgment upon Israel's oppressors.

Daniel is the most recently written book in the Hebrew Bible and the Protestant Old Testament, but the Bibles used by Roman Catholics and by Orthodox Christians include other writings from this same period (see the chart on p. 33). After Daniel was written, a group of Jews led by Judah Maccabee successfully recaptured the temple and purified it in 164 B.C. Soon they regained control of the country and set up their own government, the first independent government since Jerusalem had been conquered by the Babylonians four hundred years earlier. These events are recounted in the books of 1 and 2 Maccabees. During this period the inspiring tales of Tobit and Judith were popular. The wise sayings collected in the book known as Sirach or Ecclesiasticus became a useful educational tool. A book called the Wisdom of Solomon was composed in Egypt, exhorting people to live godly lives because those who were righteous would inherit immortality.

The books in the Old Testament were written over a span of nearly a thousand years. They provide a panoramic view of God's dealings with his people over many centuries. These texts celebrate the wonder of God's creation and the joy of Israel's liberation from slavery. They portray the anguish of Israel's apostasy and God's own relentless quest to win his people back again, by disciplining them in exile and graciously liberating them once more. Through its stories and songs, prophecies and proverbs, the Old Testament bears witness to the faithfulness of God and helps people in every age discern what it means to be God's own people.

4

How Was the New Testament Formed?

The world of the New Testament, like that of the Old, can seem like a strange and distant place, far removed from the realities of modern life. The Gospels are populated by groups of Pharisees who became irritated by seemingly benign practices like plucking a few grains of wheat on the sabbath. Lepers clad in rags toiled along the byways to Jesus and demons made people writhe and cry out at his feet. The letters written by the apostle Paul echo the concerns of Christians living amid the clatter of Roman chariots and merchants hawking their wares outside the shrines of pagan gods and goddesses. Christians were confronted by issues such as whether it was proper to eat meat offered to idols, how a slave owner should deal with a runaway slave, and whether women and men should worship with their heads covered or uncovered.

Yet the stories from this ancient world have continued to speak across the generations. Those who read the New Testament today are invited to enter its world to discover the richness of its message. By listening to the ways these texts addressed the people living in the first century, we can better discern how they continue to speak today. A sketch of the turbulent world in which the New Testament was forged is a useful way to become familiar with these texts.

The New Testament World

The winds of change that began when Alexander the Great conquered Palestine in 330 B.C. continued to shape the cultural climate for centuries. Although the Maccabees had rebelled against leaders who had gone too far in embracing Greek culture, the kingdom they founded became increasingly secular. The Romans extended their influence westward through the old Greek Empire. In 63 B.C. a Roman general conquered Jerusalem, strode into the temple, and brought two centuries of Jewish independence to an end.

The Romans eventually designated a man named Herod to rule Palestine. An ambitious and masterful politician, Herod accommodated devout Jews by transforming the modest Jerusalem temple that had been rebuilt after the exile into an imposing structure of gleaming white limestone adorned with gold. At the same time he built cities named for Caesar Augustus that contained stadiums, theaters, and temples to the emperor. After Herod died in 4 B.C., one of his sons retained control of Galilee in the north, but the regions of Samaria and Judea to the south were soon placed under a Roman governor.

Most of the people living in Judea and Galilee were Jewish. They recognized the authority of the Jewish law and periodically traveled to Jerusalem to worship in the temple. A few of the Jews belonged to distinct groups or sects. The *Sadduccees* were a priestly group who conducted the temple rituals, recognized the authority of only the first five books of the Bible, and rejected the idea of resurrection, since that was not mentioned in the Pentateuch. The *Pharisees* were a fellowship group that revered the temple and prepared meals in their homes according to the stringent standards of purity normally followed only by temple priests. The Pharisees were steeped in the written law and an extensive body of oral tradition, and believed that there would be a resurrection of the dead, an idea found in some of the more recent Old Testament writings.

Other groups included the *Essenes*, who were mainly celibate Jewish men, some of whom lived in a communal settlement near the Dead Sea. They observed rigorous standards of purity and boycotted the Jerusalem temple because they thought its priests

Chronology of the New Testament

Based on information found in the Bible and in other ancient sources, it is possible to reconstruct a general chronology of New Testament events and approximate dates for the completion of biblical books.

	Approximate Dates	People and Events	A Sample of New Testament Books
1. Roman Period Begins	63 B.C.	Romans enter Jerusalem; Herodian family given power; Roman governors appointed	
2. Jesus' Life	about 5 B.C. —A.D. 30	Birth in Bethlehem; Three-year public ministry, crucifixion, resurrection	Accounts of Jesus' teachings and ministry circulate orally
3. Early Christian Missions	A.D. 30–66	Jesus' disciples, Paul and others Gospel preached to Jews and Gentiles; Churches established from Jerusalem to Rome	Paul's letters
4. Jewish Revolt	A.D. 66–70	Jews in Palestine revolt against Rome; Temple destroyed	Mark
5. Shaping Christian Identity	A.D. 70–90	Christianity becomes increasingly distinct from Judaism; the first generation of disciples dies out	Matthew, Luke–Acts, John
6. Establishing the Christian community	A.D. 90–100	Consolidation of teaching, patterns of community life continue developing	1, 2 Timothy, Titus, 1, 2, 3 John, Revelation

were not properly authorized. The *Samaritans*, who lived in the middle of the country, were people of mixed ancestry. They recognized the authority of the Pentateuch, but rejected the Jerusalem temple, preferring to worship at a mountain called Gerizim. From time to time bands of insurgents, known as *Zealots*, plagued the Roman occupation forces, vowing to obey God alone and seeking Jewish independence.

Many of the Jews of Palestine hoped that God would send them a new leader, who was sometimes known as the "messiah" or "christ." These words mean "the anointed one" in the Hebrew and Greek languages, respectively. The Essenes anticipated the coming of two "anointed ones": a priest and a king. Others looked for the arrival of a prophet like Moses, since God had promised Moses, "I will raise up for them a prophet like you from among their own people" (Deuteronomy 18:18). Many expected a royal messiah, a new King David, who would throw off the yoke of Roman domination, restore the kingdom of Israel, and rule in peace and justice. Occasionally leaders arose who claimed to be the fulfillment of Israel's hopes, but they were soon silenced by the Roman army.

Jesus of Nazareth

It was into this unsettled world that Jesus was born, shortly before the death of Herod the Great in 4 B.C. (The people who devised the calendar we use miscalculated the time of Jesus' birth by a few years.) Jesus was born in Bethlehem in Judea, the village of King David. His mother was Mary, who was married to a man named Joseph. Jesus' childhood was spent in the northern hill country of Galilee in an obscure village called Nazareth (see Map 4). Jesus' public ministry probably began about A.D. 27 after he was baptized by John the Baptist, a fiery preacher who summoned people to repent of their sins before the coming of the Lord's judgment. The precise order of the events that followed is not certain, since none of the Gospels (Matthew, Mark, Luke, and John) preserves a complete account of Jesus' ministry, and their accounts differ from each other in some respects. Nevertheless, the main contours of his ministry seem clear.

Jesus was a teacher and a preacher who announced the coming of God's gracious rule. "The time is fulfilled, and the kingdom of God has come near; repent, and believe in the good news" (Mark 1:15). The coming of the kingdom would mean defeat for the powers of evil and joyous liberation for the people they had held captive. Yet the kingdom would not arrive with the rattling of sabers or the thunder of hoofbeats; it would grow like the leaven in a lump of dough or branches sprouting from a tiny mustard seed (Matthew 13:31-33). Jesus compared God to a shepherd combing the hillsides for a sheep that had strayed, a woman scouring her house to recover a missing coin, and a father running to embrace a long-lost son (Luke 15). God was like the host of a banquet, bringing the maimed and the blind to dine at his feast after the people he first invited refused to come (Luke 14:15-24).

Jesus' actions bore out his message. He was known for his power to release people from the afflictions of leprosy, paralysis, and blindness. Those who had been possessed by demons that made them cry out and writhe uncontrollably were liberated when Jesus cast out the demons. Tax collectors were despised for their graft and complicity with the Roman authorities, but Jesus was willing to eat with them, saying, "Those who are well have no need of a physician, but those who are sick; I have come to call not the righteous but sinners" (Mark 2:17).

Some people were drawn to Jesus and a group of followers formed. The inner circle was a group of twelve that included some who were fishermen like Peter, James, and John, but the wider circle of disciples included many other men and women. Opposition to Jesus arose, especially among the Pharisees and other religious authorities. They acknowledged that Jesus had the power to perform miracles, but charged that he spurned the law of God by healing on the Sabbath, when no work was to be done. They argued that Jesus' claims to be carrying out the work of God were scandalous; they charged that his miraculous powers came from Satan, not God (Mark 3:1-6, 22). The leaders also feared that Jesus' popularity among the people would precipitate a revolt against Rome, threatening the security of the nation.

The crisis peaked when Jesus went to Jerusalem to celebrate the Passover festival in the spring of about A.D. 30. Crowds of worshipers thronged around him as he entered the city, but one of his disciples, named Judas, collaborated with the authorities to have him arrested. On Thursday evening Jesus ate a final meal with his disciples and went to a garden near Jerusalem. There he was seized, taken to the house of the high priest, and questioned. On Friday morning he was brought before Pilate, the Roman governor, and charged with claiming to be a king. He was stripped, beaten, and hung on a cross where he died later that same day. His body was placed in a nearby tomb cut in rock.

On Sunday morning several women discovered that the tomb was open and that Jesus' body was gone. They were greeted by an angel who announced that Jesus had risen; some accounts add that the women saw the risen Jesus himself. Soon Jesus appeared to groups of his followers who testified that he was alive. The appearances of the risen Christ eventually ended, but the proclamation of his life, death, and resurrection continued through the work of his disciples.

Paul and the Early Church

The story of Jesus was not written down right away, but spread through early Christian preaching (see the chart on p. 43). The disciples both preserved and interpreted the tradition they received. They sought out connections between the Old Testament writings and the events of Jesus' life, death, and resurrection in order to help people understand the gospel message. Many Jewish people were expecting a messiah who would inaugurate a kingdom like that of King David, not one who would be executed on a cross. The Scriptures even said that someone who was killed by being hung on a tree was cursed by God (Deuteronomy 21:22-23); therefore they were certain that Jesus could not be God's messiah. The early disciples began to counter such objections by showing that Jesus actually fulfilled the promises made in the Old Testament.

The belief that Jesus would return in a short time gave great urgency to the spread of the gospel, and many people were gripped by the good news about Jesus. Enlivened by the Spirit of God, they gathered in homes for prayer and fellowship. Many of the religious authorities opposed the new faith and some of Jesus' followers were imprisoned or killed. Others fled to places outside

Judea, where the gospel message was received by Samaritans and Greeks as well as by Jews.

One of the Jewish leaders who persecuted the emerging church was Saul of Tarsus, better known to us as the apostle Paul. Near the city of Damascus he encountered the risen Christ, who called him to be a proclaimer of rather than an adversary of the gospel. Paul set out on a career as a missionary, proclaiming the message of Jesus Christ in the cities of what is now Syria, Turkey, and Greece (see Map 5). He became a leading figure in the mission to non-Jewish people, who were known as Gentiles. His preaching centered on a vivid proclamation of Jesus the crucified Messiah, a message that kindled faith in the hearts of many hearers who were stirred by the power of the Holy Spirit (1 Corinthians 2:1-5; Galatians 3:1-3).

The letters Paul wrote during the latter part of his ministry (A.D. 50–60) are the oldest Christian writings we know about. They were written in Greek and have been arranged according to their length in our present New Testament, with the longest letters first and the shorter letters last. As you read Paul's letters, look for clues to the main themes in the first chapter of each one. Note Paul's comments about the intended recipients of each letter and the tone of his writing. Some of Paul's arguments are difficult to follow, but the main points are usually clear.

The oldest of the letters is probably 1 Thessalonians, written about A.D. 50. It begins with a warm reminder of how eagerly the Thessalonians had embraced the gospel and how they awaited the return of Christ in glory (1:1-10). Later, Paul indicated that the Thessalonians were grieving the death of some of their members and he assured them that since Jesus died and rose they could be sure that Christians who died would also rise (4:13-14).

At Galatia, some visiting evangelists were stirring up the congregations, apparently insisting that the Galatian Christians needed to eat kosher food and observe Jewish holidays and that the males be circumcised according to Jewish law. They warned that those who did not keep these laws were not true people of God. Paul wrote a pointed response, reminding them that people enter a right relationship with God through faith in Christ, not by observing the Jewish law. Therefore, Christians also *live* by faith in Christ, not by the Jewish law (Galatians 2:16-20).

The Corinthians were a quarrelsome group who had split up into factions. When Paul heard about it, he sent a letter asking, "Has Christ been divided? Was Paul crucified for you? Or were you baptized in the name of Paul?" (1 Corinthians 1:13). Certainly not! Paul therefore called them back to the unity they already

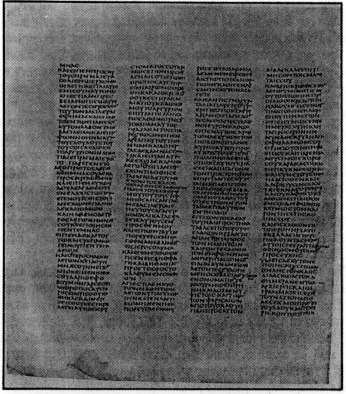

A section of the New Testament from the fourth century Greek manuscript known as Codex Sinaiticus.

shared in Jesus Christ. The letter known as 2 Corinthians was sent later, strengthening ties between Paul and the congregation.

Paul was imprisoned because of his missionary activities. While in prison he wrote a warm letter to the Philippians, thanking them for supporting him. He rejoiced at the spread of the gospel of Christ Jesus, who had been crucified and exalted by the power of God, "that at the name of Jesus every knee should bend . . . and every tongue should confess that Jesus Christ is Lord" (Philippians 2:10-11). Paul also wrote to a man named Philemon, asking that he receive back a runaway slave as a brother in Christ.

The last letter from Paul that we know about was probably his letter to the Romans, written around A.D. 55–57. Paul hoped for an opportunity to preach to the Christians in Rome and his letter provided them with an extended summary of his message before his arrival. In it he declared, "I am not ashamed of the gospel; it is the power of God for salvation to everyone who has faith, to the Jew first and also to the Greek" (Romans 1:16). The book of Acts tells us that Paul eventually was taken to Rome as a prisoner. Later Christian writings also say he was executed there because of his Christian faith.

The Gospels and Acts

Paul's letters contain almost no information about Jesus' teaching or his life, apart from comments about his death and resurrection. The accounts of Jesus' life and teachings circulated for decades by word of mouth. As the stories were told and retold, they were shaped into standard patterns that made them easier to remember. Miracle stories usually identified the setting in which the miracle took place (a synagogue, home, or boat) and the problem that confronted Jesus (a person possessed by demons, an illness, or a storm), then described his miraculous response to the problem and the crowd's amazement at his power. Such stories were probably told to help evoke the same positive response to Jesus from the listeners as the original miracle had drawn from observers. Stories about Jesus' conflicts with the Jewish authorities typically began by stating the setting of the encounter, a question or challenge made by Jesus' opponents, and Jesus' reply. These stories were probably told to help Christians respond to the challenges confronting them in their own lives.

The Gospel of Mark is the oldest of the four Gospels, written down about A.D. 65–70 or roughly forty years after the time of Jesus (see the chart on p. 43). The opening chapters reflect the oral shaping of the material on which this gospel is based. Chapter

1 includes miracle stories that follow the pattern noted above (1:21-28, 29-31, 40-45), and chapter 2 contains a series of conflict stories that also follow the typical pattern (2:15-17, 18-22, 23-28). Christians in the second century said that this gospel was produced by a man named Mark who based it on the preaching of Peter. Although this tradition is not certain, the impact of early Christian preaching on the book is clear.

As you read Mark's Gospel you will discover that it is not simply a collection of stories, but a compelling drama. In the beginning Jesus was baptized by John the Baptist, only to be hurled immediately into conflict with the powers of evil. He was tempted by Satan in the wilderness and prevailed. He summoned disciples to follow him as if he were a general marshaling his troops. He cast out demons from those who were possessed, but both the Jewish authorities and his own disciples misunderstood the nature of his power. Only when Jesus hung on the cross, crying out, "My God, my God, why have you forsaken me," (Mark 15:34) would it become clear what it meant to call Jesus the Son of God. The women who visited the tomb were told that Jesus was alive, but they fled from the tomb and "said nothing to anyone, for they were afraid" (Mark 16:8).

Mark's disquieting story of the suffering Messiah would have startled the Christians of his time into grasping the faith more firmly. It would have reminded them that God's power is made known in suffering, that Christ's victory comes through apparent defeat, and that silence about his resurrection cannot be the last word. At the time Mark wrote, Judea was being swept into a conflict with Rome that would culminate in the destruction of Jerusalem and its temple in A.D. 70. Mark's Gospel would have helped Christians persevere in the faith despite the realities of suffering and death.

The Gospels of Matthew and Luke were written somewhat later, about A.D. 85, after Jerusalem had been destroyed and the Jewish people were adjusting to life without a temple. Christians in the second century thought that Matthew's Gospel was written by one of the twelve disciples and Luke's Gospel by a companion of Paul, although this is unlikely. Both Matthew and Luke reproduced portions of Mark's Gospel, adding independent accounts of Jesus' birth and resurrection appearances. Both also drew on a collection of Jesus' sayings that had been compiled sometime before, creating fresh accounts of Jesus' ministry for their time.

As you read Matthew's Gospel you will find that it is a carefully crafted narrative. The opening chapters trace Jesus' ancestry back to Abraham, pointing out how the events surrounding his birth fulfilled passages of the Old Testament. Matthew also observed that the first people to worship the infant Jesus were not Jews but wise men from the east, and that Jesus was the light to the Gentiles promised in Scripture (4:12-17). Jesus' public ministry begins with a lengthy collection of sayings that establish his teaching authority over that of the scribes (chapters 5-7) and concludes with him making charges against the Jewish leaders (chapter 23). When he appeared after his resurrection, Jesus commanded his disciples to teach and make disciples of all nations. Matthew's portrait of Jesus firmly anchored the church's teaching and mission in the tradition of Israel, despite opposition from those who were rebuilding the Jewish community after the fall of Jerusalem (see Matthew 28:11-15).

The Gospel of Luke also stresses the continuity between the church and Israel. The figures who appear in the opening chapters include the aged and devout parents of John the Baptist, together with Simeon and Anna, two righteous Israelites who joyously greeted the arrival of the Christ child when Mary and Joseph brought him to the temple. Jesus' ministry begins with him reading from the Scriptures and claiming to fulfill them (4:16-21). His mission drew him relentlessly on to Jerusalem, to be killed like the prophets of old (13:33-35). The Holy Spirit was the driving force in Jesus' ministry, and the Gospel concludes with the disciples in the temple, awaiting the Spirit's next move (24:49-53). The book of Acts is the sequel to the story, tracing how the Spirit empowered the disciples to proclaim the gospel "in Jerusalem, in all Judea and Samaria, and to the ends of the earth" (Acts 1:8).

The Gospel of John presents an account of Jesus' ministry based on the testimony of "the disciple whom Jesus loved" (John 21:20-24). Although his name is not given in the Gospel, Christians in the second century thought he was John, one of Jesus' twelve disciples. The soaring poetry of the opening chapter takes readers back to the dawn of time, when God created the world by the power of the Word. That creative Word became flesh in the person of Jesus (John 1:1-18). Jesus manifested his divine power by turning water into wine and raising Lazarus from the dead, but his claims to have come from God were rejected as blasphemy. He was hung on a cross, but there revealed the fullness of God's self-giving love by laying down his life for the world that had hated him. The Gospel's heated disputes and vivid symbols of light, darkness, water, and bread present a compelling message that would have helped secure the faith of Christians against the opposition of an unbelieving world.

Later Writings

As the first century drew to a close, the first generation of disciples died out. Christians of subsequent generations brought the legacy of the earlier disciples to bear on their changing situations, and some of these writings appear in the New Testament (see the chart on p. 43). The letters of 1, 2, and 3 John were written in the wake of a split within the Christian community. The author took readers back to the tradition they had received "from the beginning" in the hope of restoring fellowship (1 John 1:1-4). The letters of 1 and 2 Timothy and Titus are attributed to Paul, but were probably written by someone who brought Paul's authority to bear on issues such as the selection of bishops and deacons and the need to safeguard Christian teachings against heresy.

Several of the later New Testament writings were intended to give encouragement to Christians whose enthusiasm for the faith was waning. The book of Hebrews compares Christians to the people of Israel, who journeyed in the wilderness for many years. It urges them to persevere in the certainty that God has prepared a place of blessed rest for them. The book of James cautions that faith cannot be reduced to a set of comfortable beliefs, insisting that genuine faith is expressed in actions. The book of 1 Peter assured Christians who were suffering that God was preserving them in faith for the salvation that was theirs in Jesus Christ.

Finally, the book of Revelation presents a vivid glimpse into the struggles of seven congregations late in the first century, about A.D. 95–96. Some were plagued by false teachings, others suffered persecution, and two had become lethargic because of their own prosperity (Revelation 2–3). Those who read Revelation should ask what the warnings and hopes contained in its visions would have meant to the seven churches to whom the book was addressed. Readers who listen to how the book spoke to churches in the late first century can better discern ways it can speak to people today.

The books of the New Testament take readers on a journey through the ministry of Jesus and the formation of the early church. The texts capture the exuberance of the crowds who awaited Jesus' healing touch and the horror of Jesus' arrest, trial, and crucifixion. They depict the astonishment of the disciples who witnessed the resurrection and provide glimpses into the joys and challenges confronting the community of faith. Through stories, songs, and letters, the New Testament bears witness to the love of God in Jesus Christ and helps Christians of every time and place understand what it means to be Jesus' disciples.

5

Who Decided
Which Books Belong
in the Bible?

The Bibles we use today have a fixed table of contents beginning with Genesis and ending with Revelation. The books of the Bible are bound together between the covers of a single volume and seem to form a well-defined collection. But when Protestants compare their Bibles with those used by Roman Catholics and Orthodox Christians, problems appear immediately. Protestants count thirty-nine books in their Old Testament, while Roman Catholics have forty-six books and the Eastern Orthodox churches include forty-nine or fifty books in their Old Testaments. Those who browse the shelves of Bibles in a bookstore may find two editions of the same Bible placed side by side; a shorter edition next to a longer edition bearing the words "with the Apocrypha" on the cover. The term *apocrypha* refers to the extra books contained in Roman Catholic and Orthodox Bibles.

The books in the Bible form an authoritative collection or *canon* ("rule" or "standard") for Christian faith and teaching. Christians have always confessed that supreme authority belongs to God; they have also recognized that some writings bear faithful witness to God while others do not. Over a period of centuries the Christian community identified a collection of books that provide a standard for true witness to God. The fact that Christian groups differ concerning the number of books included in their Bibles means that their standards for true teaching differ somewhat. A sketch of the development of the biblical canon can help show how the differences came about and what it means to read the Bible as a book distinct from other books.

Formation of the Old Testament Canon

The writings found in the Old Testament were composed over a long period of time, as we noted in chapter 3, and each one was written on a separate scroll. Many other texts circulated alongside these writings. For example, there were collections of poems like the Book of the Wars of the Lord (mentioned in Numbers 21:14) and the book of Jashar (Joshua 10:13; 2 Samuel 1:18), and books recording the deeds of Israel's kings (1 Kings 11:41; 14:19). All of these writings have now been lost. Eventually the community of faith identified a few of the many texts available as standards for their corporate faith and teachings.

The first collection of books that acquired special authoritative status for Israel was the Law or Pentateuch (discussed in chapter 2 of this book). The importance of a central document for the community emerged by the time of Josiah (621 B.C.), when a text that was probably our book of Deuteronomy was adopted as the basis for reforming Israel's worship (2 Kings 22–23). The destruction of Jerusalem and the Exile to Babylonia in 586 B.C. meant that the people had to organize their community's life without a temple or their own independent government. The traditional laws of Israel became the focal point that enabled the Jewish people to exist as a distinct community under foreign domination.

During the Exile and the period just after the Exile, writings were collected and edited into the books we know as the Pentateuch, Genesis through Deuteronomy. The scribes Ezra and Nehemiah publicly read all or parts of these books during their efforts to rebuild the Jewish community that had returned to Palestine (Nehemiah 8). By 400 B.C. the Pentateuch had become established as a charter for the Jewish people, containing the traditions and ordinances that identified them as a community. In subsequent centuries the Pentateuch was translated into Greek and used in Jewish communities throughout the ancient world.

Despite the deep divisions that emerged between Jews and Samaritans, and between different Jewish groups such as the Pharisees and Sadducees, all recognized the authority of the five books of the Torah or Law.

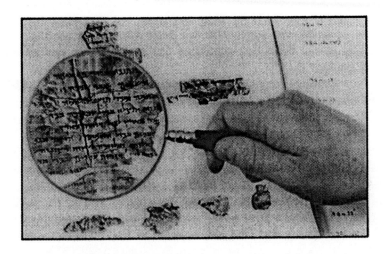

Fragments from the Dead Sea scrolls discovered in
caves near Qumran in Israel in 1947.

The second group of writings to be recognized as authoritative for the community were the books of the prophets. The "former prophets" were the books of Joshua, Judges, Samuel, and Kings, which included stories about prophets such as Elijah and Elisha, as well as Israel's other leaders. These writings demonstrated the importance of the ordinances found in Deuteronomy for Israel's life as a people. The "latter prophets" included the books of Isaiah, Jeremiah, Ezekiel, and the twelve Minor Prophets, Hosea through Malachi. These writings helped strengthen the community by showing how God had dealt faithfully with Israel's forebears, calling for obedience on the part of the people, and maintaining a vision of hope for their future. By 200 B.C. most Jews recognized the authority of both the Law and the Prophets.

The third group of texts to be included among Israel's sacred Scriptures was simply called "the Writings." These included the Psalms, Proverbs, and Job, five books that were read on various Jewish festivals (the Song of Solomon, Ruth, Lamentations, Ecclesiastes, and Esther), the book of Daniel, and several historical writings (Ezra, Nehemiah, and Chronicles). Many of these texts were highly esteemed by Jews in the second century B.C., but their authoritative status and the exact number of writings included in the collection remained unclear until the end of the first century A.D.

New writings continued to be produced by Jews of this period, and these circulated alongside the writings listed above. The book of Sirach, later known as Ecclesiasticus, was written about 180 B.C., was translated into Greek, and enjoyed a wide popularity among Jews of Palestine and Egypt. The story of Judith was an inspiring tale about a pious widow who delivered a city from the Babylonian army. Writings such as 1 Enoch and the Testament of Moses contained visions about the coming end of the world order. The Essene Jews living near the Dead Sea maintained an extensive library that was rediscovered in 1947. These writings, known as the Dead Sea Scrolls, included nearly all the books in our Old Testament, along with many texts not found in the Bible, such as a collection of hymns, regulations for Essene community life, and a vision of a future war between the sons of light and the sons of darkness.

After Jerusalem was destroyed by the Romans in A.D. 70, a group of Pharisees and rabbis began reorganizing the Jewish community at a place called Jamnia near the Mediterranean coast of Palestine. There they established an academy for the study and practice of Jewish law. About A.D. 90 the rabbis who taught there determined that the authoritative writings should be limited to the books in what is now the Hebrew Bible and the Protestant Old Testament, although some wanted to omit the Song of Solomon and Ecclesiastes, and others wanted to include Sirach. These Jewish leaders, however, did not have the power to decree which books should be in the Bible or to impose their views on Jews elsewhere. Instead, their deliberations were a final phase in the long process through which the Jewish community reached a consensus about the writings it considered authoritative.

Jesus' ministry took place earlier in the first century (about A.D. 27–30), at a time when the status of some of the sacred writings was uncertain. He referred most often to "the Law and the Prophets," but did quote passages from other writings as well, especially the Psalms. As Christianity spread outside of Palestine, the Greek translation of the Old Testament quickly became the Bible of the church. The exact number of books included in the Greek Bible apparently remained in flux for some time. Eventually it came to include not only the books found in the Jewish Scriptures and Protestant Old Testament, but also the additional books found in Roman Catholic and Orthodox Bibles today.

Christians organized the books in their Old Testament into a sequence that reflected their Christian faith (see the chart on p. 60). The Jewish Scriptures begin with the five books of the Law, then the Prophets, and conclude with the Writings. The last book in Hebrew Bibles is 2 Chronicles, which ends with the king of Persia announcing that he would build a new temple and inviting all Jews to go up to Jerusalem. Christians, however, placed the prophetic books last, so that the Old Testament ends with the promise that Elijah the prophet would appear before the day of the Lord arrived (Malachi 4:5-6). This promise anticipates the gospel narratives about John the Baptist, who fulfilled the role of Elijah and prepared people for the coming of Christ.

The debate over which books belong in the Old Testament has periodically been renewed among Christians. The Latin Bible, known as the Vulgate, was based on the longer Greek Old Testament, although Jerome, one of the translators, wanted to follow the shorter Hebrew canon and place the extra Old Testament books in a separate category. In the sixteenth century, Martin Luther's German translation did place the extra books in a separate collection called the "Apocrypha," which means "hidden." Luther granted that the apocryphal books were useful to read, but denied that they could establish true teaching, especially since the medieval church had tied the idea of purgatory to 2 Maccabees 12:43-45. The English *King James Version* originally contained the Apocrypha, but these books were dropped in later printings.

Protestants have continued to insist that authoritative teachings cannot be based on the apocryphal books, although the Church of England occasionally reads selections from these writings in

Books Included in the Old Testament

All major Christian traditions and denominations include the thirty-nine books of the Hebrew Bible as part of the Old Testament canon. Roman Catholics also include seven books of the Apocrypha, and Eastern Orthodox Christians include a few others.

Hebrew Bible (39 books)	Protestant Old Testament (39 books)	Roman Catholic Old Testament (46 books)
Torah	*Pentateuch*	*Pentateuch*
Genesis	Genesis	Genesis
Exodus	Exodus	Exodus
Leviticus	Leviticus	Leviticus
Numbers	Numbers	Numbers
Deuteronomy	Deuteronomy	Deuteronomy
Former Prophets		
Joshua	*History*	*History*
Judges	Joshua	Joshua
1 and 2 Samuel	Judges	Judges
1 and 2 Kings	Ruth	Ruth
	1 and 2 Samuel	1 and 2 Samuel
Later Prophets	1 and 2 Kings	1 and 2 Kings
Isaiah	1 and 2 Chronicles	1 and 2 Chronicles
Jeremiah	Ezra	Ezra
Ezekiel	Nehemiah	Nehemiah
Hosea	Esther	Tobit
Joel		Judith
Amos	*Wisdom*	Esther (longer form)
Obadiah	Job	1 and 2 Maccabees
Jonah	Psalms	
Micah	Proverbs	*Wisdom*
Nahum	Ecclesiastes	Job
Habakkuk	Song of Solomon	Psalms
Zephaniah		Proverbs
Haggai	*Prophets*	Ecclesiastes
Zechariah	Isaiah	Song of Solomon
Malachi	Jeremiah	Wisdom of Solomon
	Lamentations	Sirach (Ecclesiasticus)
Writings	Ezekiel	
Psalms	Daniel	*Prophets*
Job	Hosea	Isaiah
Proverbs	Joel	Jeremiah
Ruth	Amos	Lamentations
Song of Solomon	Obadiah	Baruch
Ecclesiastes	Jonah	Ezekiel
Lamentations	Micah	Daniel (longer form)
Esther	Nahum	Hosea
Daniel	Habakkuk	Joel
Ezra	Zephaniah	Amos
Nehemiah	Haggai	Obadiah
1 and 2 Chronicles	Zechariah	Jonah
	Malachi	Micah
		Nahum
		Habakkuk
		Zephaniah
		Haggai
		Zechariah
		Malachi

its worship services. The Roman Catholic Church reaffirmed the authority of both the Old Testament and the Apocrypha in 1546. The editions of the Old Testament used by Eastern Orthodox churches also contain the apocryphal books, plus a number of other writings not found in Protestant Bibles. The Russian Orthodox church includes Psalm 151, 1 and 2 Esdras, and 3 Maccabees. The Greek Orthodox church omits 2 Esdras, but includes the Prayer of Manasseh and prints 4 Maccabees as an appendix.

Formation of the New Testament Canon

The first Christians proclaimed Jesus' death and resurrection and passed on his teaching by word of mouth. The sacred writings they read aloud at their gatherings were the Jewish scriptures, that is, the Old Testament. Occasionally letters were sent to Christian communities from missionaries like Paul, with the request that "this letter be read to all of them" (1 Thessalonians 5:27). Some of the more important letters were preserved and read again when the community assembled; occasionally copies were made for other congregations.

Time passed and the first generation of disciples began dying out. The church's mission spread to the far-flung corners of the Roman Empire. It became vital to preserve the testimony of Jesus' first followers and to provide accounts of his life and teachings for the congregations of a growing church. Gospels were written, circulated, and revised. By the end of the first century a given congregation might have had access to a collection of Paul's letters, one or more of the Gospels, and perhaps some of the other Christian writings in circulation at the time. It was also becoming more common for Christian writings to be read aloud alongside the Jewish Scriptures when Christians gathered for worship.

In the second century new religious movements arose that threatened the young church. A man named Marcion, who had once been a Christian, taught that the world was an evil place created by the vengeful God he thought was depicted by the Jewish Scriptures; he claimed that a "higher" God sent Jesus to rescue people from the evils of the world. He rejected the Old Testament altogether and formed his own collection of Christian writings to support his claims. These included the letters of Paul, which did include arguments against the saving power of the law of Moses, and an edited version of the Gospel of Luke, which Marcion thought had been composed by one of Paul's companions. Later, a self-proclaimed prophet named Montanus declared that the end of the world was at hand and that a new age of the Spirit had dawned. The fervor he aroused won many converts and spawned a number of writings that helped to spread his teachings.

In response to these challenges, Christians identified a number of writings that provided a standard for authentic Christian teaching and preaching. About A.D. 185, Irenaeus, the bishop of Lyons in southern France, taught that the authoritative writings were the four Gospels, Acts, and the letters of Paul. He had two reasons for singling out these texts. First, he understood that they preserved the preaching of the apostles, even though the apostles themselves did not actually write all of them. Second, their content was sound: they taught that there was one God, the Creator of heaven and earth, who is proclaimed in the Jewish Scriptures, and that Jesus Christ is the Son of God. Other leaders of his time agreed, adding that these writings were the ones actually used in Christian congregations at that time.

Irenaeus also knew of other writings that were highly regarded by Christians. These were 1 Peter, 1 and 2 John, Revelation, and probably Hebrews, all of which were later included in the Christian canon, as well as a letter from Clement, bishop of Rome, and a collection of visions, admonitions, and parables known as the Shepherd of Hermas. Some Christians also had high regard for the Apocalypse of Peter, which contained teachings about the end of the world and visions of the last judgment, together with the letter of Jude, which is found in our New Testament. Surprisingly, the books of James, 2 Peter, and 3 John, which appear in our New Testaments, were not mentioned among the authoritative texts used by Christians in the late second century.

As the third century dawned, the core collection of New Testament books was well-established but its boundaries remained fluid. Religious groups such as the Gnostics, who claimed to have a special knowledge of salvation, produced writings that both resembled and threatened Christian teachings. For example, the Gospel of Thomas claimed to have been written by an apostle. It began, "These are the secret words which the living Jesus spoke, and which Didymus Judas Thomas wrote." The book contained familiar sayings of Jesus, like the parables about a sower planting seeds and a merchant discovering a fine pearl. It also likened the world to a corpse and concluded by saying that although women cannot be saved, "every woman who makes herself a male will enter the kingdom of heaven." People wondered if such a book should be used for Christian teaching and preaching.

The Christian writers Origen and Eusebius provide glimpses into the way the Christian community finally defined its list of authoritative writings in the third and fourth centuries. The first criterion was that a book should be used throughout the whole church, not just in isolated congregations. The second criterion was that a book's contents should be consistent with the community's consensus about true Christian teaching. The third criterion was that a book should preserve the teaching of the first apostles, even though an apostle need not actually have written it. Books like the Gospel of Thomas claimed to have been written by an apostle, but were rejected because of their contents and use by sectarian religious groups.

The church in Europe and North Africa reached agreement about the books of the New Testament in the fourth century. The four Gospels, Acts, the letters of Paul, Hebrews, 1 John, and 1 Peter were firmly accepted. Some uncertainties persisted about James, 2 Peter, 2 and 3 John, Jude, and Revelation, but by A.D. 367, the bishop of Alexandria in Egypt could say that all of these writings were accepted as authoritative for the church. Christians in Syria still preferred to use a book that combined all the Gospels into a single account of Jesus' life instead of using the four separate Gospels. They also used the book of Acts and the letters of Paul, plus a book known as 3 Corinthians. In the fifth century the Syrian church adopted most of the New Testament books used by the church in the west, but remained ambivalent about 2 Peter, 2 and 3 John, Jude, and Revelation.

The debate about the boundaries of the New Testament subsided, only to erupt again during the Reformation in the sixteenth century. Martin Luther declared that the heart of the scriptures was that Jesus Christ saves people from sin, death, and the devil, and that the gift of salvation is received by faith. He insisted that some of the books of the New Testament proclaimed this message more effectively than others. In his "Preface to the Epistles of St. James and St. Jude" he wrote, "And that is the true test by which to judge all books, when we see whether or not they inculcate Christ" (*Luther's Works*, vol. 35, Fortress Press, p. 396). In Luther's eyes the books of Hebrews, James, Jude, and Revelation did not proclaim Christ clearly enough, but since they had long been used in the church, he simply relegated them to the very end of his German translation of the New Testament. The Reformed and Roman Catholic churches, however, reaffirmed the authoritative status of these books and continued to print them in their traditional order. This practice is followed in English Bibles today.

Reading the Bible As Canon

When you open the Bible you will read books that have proven their value to the community of faith over many centuries. The books of the Bible were not chosen by a committee or imposed on Christians and Jews by their leaders. The writings included in the Bible are those that were actually used by the people of God in generation after generation. The selection of these writings from the many texts produced by Jews, Christians, and other religious groups reflects the collective wisdom of the community of faith. They identified a group of writings that bore faithful witness to God and set a standard for authentic Christian teaching and preaching.

The history of this process suggests that some books of the Bible are more important than others. The Jewish community recognized the value of Genesis long before it accepted the book of Ecclesiastes. Christians gave a central place to the four Gospels and the letters of Paul long before they received 2 Peter into the canon. Protestants and Roman Catholics agree on the importance of thirty-nine Old Testament books, but disagree about the status of others. Consciously or unconsciously, Christians continue to turn to some books of the Bible much more often than others; the Psalms and the Gospel of John are usually more well-thumbed than Obadiah and Jude, for example. As you read the Bible, you too will discover passages that seem especially instructive, beautiful, or moving.

At the same time, readers should keep in mind that even books that seem obscure have spoken to generations of Christians in the past. A text that is of only passing interest in one generation may become compelling for a later generation. Paul's letter to the Romans was vital to the sixteenth-century reformers, who protested the demands placed on believers by the medieval church. Later, it was the story of Israel journeying through the wilderness that captured the imagination of pioneers on the American frontier. The spectrum of writings contained in the biblical library contains riches waiting to be rediscovered in each generation.

6

How Have People Viewed the Bible?

People who read the Bible usually want to understand what the ancient texts mean for life today. Some Bible passages seem to speak easily across the centuries. With little explanation the gentle words of Psalm 23, "The Lord is my shepherd, I shall not want," have assured Christians in almost every time and place. Similarly, Jesus' stories about a father welcoming home his wayward son and a Samaritan who had compassion for a man injured by robbers can be easily read and appreciated.

Other passages can be confusing and even disturbing. Revelation 13, for example, depicts a beast with seven heads and ten horns rising up from the sea to persecute the people of God. What does that passage have to do with life today? A person who reads the text may ask others what they think about it. One friend may have heard that the beast should be identified with an alliance of European countries or with the United Nations. A second friend may dismiss the text as the bizarre fantasy of a first century visionary. A third may have heard that the beast once referred to the Roman emperor but that it could also be a timeless portrait of evil.

Passages such as Revelation 13 challenge even casual readers of the Bible to think about the various ways people bring texts written two or three thousand years ago to bear on life today. They also raise the question as to whether some ways of reading the Bible are better than others. A look at some of the ways people have read and attempted to understand the Bible can help people today in their reading of it.

Old Texts for a New Time

The task of interpreting the old texts in new and changing circumstances is not new. Jewish people in the first century looked to the Scriptures as a guide for living; as times changed, their statutes had to be reinterpreted. For example, the Law mandated that animals and grain should be burned as offerings to God in Israel's central sanctuary, but the destruction of the temple in A.D. 70 made such sacrifices impossible. The rabbis who were reorganizing Judaism concluded, therefore, that study of the Law fulfilled the requirement for sacrifices. For Jews, the teachings of these rabbis and their predecessors, which were handed down orally, became the key to understanding the Scriptures.

Christians faced the problem of reinterpreting the Bible in light of a watershed in their own history: the death and resurrection of Jesus. Prior to Jesus' coming, people were familiar with biblical passages that spoke of God's messiah as a powerful king and envisioned the establishment of God's rule on earth. But after Jesus' death and resurrection, his followers began reading the Old Testament Scriptures in a new way. They understood that Jesus fulfilled passages that spoke of suffering as well those that spoke of glory. Jesus was the servant of God who suffered "like a lamb that is led to the slaughter" (Isaiah 53:7-8, cited in Acts 8:32-33) as well as the heir of the promises God made to King David (Isaiah 55:3, cited in Acts 13:34). The death of Jesus was also understood as a sacrifice that made further sacrifices unnecessary (Hebrews 9:24-26); therefore Christianity could continue to thrive despite the destruction of the Jerusalem temple.

Jesus' first followers expected him to return in glory within their lifetimes. But as the decades passed without his return, Christians began to look for a "timeless" way to read the Scriptures. Teachers such as Origen and Augustine in North Africa and Thomas Aquinas in medieval Europe developed ways of understanding the Bible on different levels. People might look to the Bible for historical information, for moral teachings, or for spiritual truths. They said that a single passage of Scripture could be read on all these levels.

To see how such an approach worked, consider the story of the cleansing of the temple. According to John 2:13-22, Jesus went up to the temple for the festival of Passover. There he found merchants selling oxen, sheep, and pigeons for sacrifices and people exchanging foreign money for local currency. Jesus made a whip and drove them out of the temple, saying, "Stop making my Father's house a marketplace." Bystanders asked him to perform a miracle to demonstrate his authority for such an outrageous action. Jesus retorted, "Destroy this temple, and in three days I will raise it up," which cryptically referred to the miracle of his own death and resurrection.

Christian interpreters explained that on the first or literal level, this text shows that sacrifices were a part of Jewish religious practice and that Jesus was attempting to correct certain abuses of the system. On the second, or moral level, Jesus warned against abuses in the church, especially against leaders who use their positions for personal gain rather than for the good of the people. On the third, or spiritual level, the story shows how Jesus drives out base and sinful desires from the soul, preparing it for salvation. Interpreters often attached spiritual significance to each detail in the story, equating the whip with Christ's Word, the oxen with earthly things, the sheep with senseless things, and the dove with empty thoughts. Such interpretations are called "allegorical"; they seem fanciful, but were accepted as long as their message was consistent with the teaching of the church.

This approach to the Bible remained popular for centuries, but in the early 1500s Martin Luther introduced a striking new way of reading the Scriptures. The church of his time taught that people could contribute to their own salvation by donating money for church buildings, making pilgrimages to Rome, and performing devotional exercises and acts of charity. Luther was plagued with doubt about his own ability to merit salvation. But as he read the Bible, he discovered passages that said salvation was a gift from God. He eventually rejected the idea that each detail of a biblical text could be given spiritual significance, and urged that people focus on the literal meaning of the text, which spoke clearly of God's gift of grace in Jesus Christ.

Luther counseled people to read the Bible in terms of its central message. He pointed out that some parts of the Bible do lay down the "law," demanding that people turn away from sin. Other parts proclaim the gospel, the good news that salvation is Christ's gracious gift, which people receive by faith. He said that the Bible's demands and words of judgment are intended to restrain the powers of sin and evil and drive people back to the gracious love

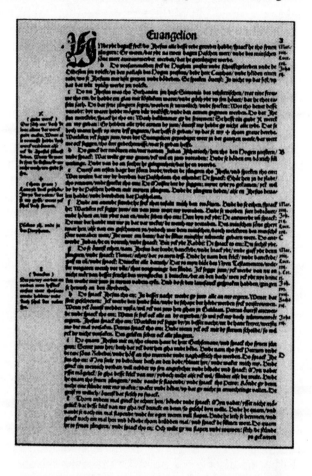

A page from Martin Luther's German translation of the Bible. He wanted to make the Bible, then available only in Latin and to priests and scholars, accessible to ordinary people.

of Christ, who is the true heart of the Bible. Luther urged that all of Scripture be understood in that light.

John Calvin was a younger contemporary of Luther who agreed that the Bible was essentially clear in its message. He maintained that people had become ignorant of God through sin, but that true knowledge of God was revealed in Scripture. He stressed that Jesus had come to restore the Law to its true spiritual purpose and urged people to read the Scriptures for instruction in living godly lives. Calvin sought to organize the church on the basis of biblical teachings, hoping that society as a whole could be brought under its moral discipline.

Calvin's approach to the Bible was brought to America by the Puritans who settled in New England. The Bible was the main book they read and they came to the New World to establish a society based on its principles. They envisioned this society in biblical terms as "a city built on a hill" (Matthew 5:14) and wanted it to set an example for peoples everywhere. As they prepared to step onto the new shores, they felt like God's people of old, poised beside the Jordan River and with the promised land in view. The words Moses spoke to Israel rang in their ears: "If you obey the commandments of the Lord your God that I am commanding you today . . . the Lord your God will bless you in the land that you are entering to possess" (Deuteronomy 30:16).

Not all the immigrants to the New World came willingly. The slave ships crossing the Atlantic brought Africans in chains to America's shores. Although few of them could read, the stories in the Bible were passed along by word of mouth, providing them with a source of inspiration and hope. The stories of Israel escaping from slavery in Egypt, Daniel being delivered from the lion's den, and three young men standing secure amid the flames of a furnace captured the imagination of the slaves and were celebrated in their songs.

As times have changed, Christians have repeatedly been challenged to read the Bible in new ways. They have asked questions arising from experiences in places as different as Roman North Africa, medieval Europe, and colonial America. The Bible has not always provided neat answers to their questions, but it has continued to assure and challenge people in ways that bring meaning to their lives.

The Bible and Church Tradition

As people in the past have reinterpreted the Bible for their own times, they have generated traditions that continue to affect the ways people read the Bible today. Jews still interpret the Bible through their oral tradition and Christians understand it in light of Christ. The two groups can often agree on what a text meant to people living centuries before Christ, but will disagree about what the text means for people today. For example, both agree that the Pentateuch prescribes offering animal sacrifices to God and yet neither group actually makes such sacrifices today. But as we noted earlier, observant Jews hold that study of the Law is now equivalent to bringing sacrifices, while Christians insist that the death of Christ makes further sacrifices unnecessary.

Roman Catholics are the heirs of the approach to Scripture that developed during the Middle Ages. The kind of allegorical interpretation we noted earlier is no longer used, but Catholics do maintain that God's will is revealed in two ways: through the Scriptures and the authoritative teachings of the church. In 1546 the Council of Trent decreed that in matters of faith and morals no one could interpret Scripture contrary to the official doctrines of the church or contradict the unanimous consensus of its recognized teachers. This position was reaffirmed by the Second Vatican Council in 1965, with the understanding that the church's teaching authority did not stand above the Scriptures, but was intended to reliably interpret the Scriptures.

The strength of this approach is that it provides stability in the ways people understand the Bible, while guarding against distorted readings of the texts. A problem with this view is the fact that church tradition itself is subject to change and sometimes needs correction. Another problem is that for many years most Roman Catholics were familiar only with the select portions of Scripture read during worship or cited in catechetical instruction. In recent decades, however, there has been a renewed interest in the Bible among many Roman Catholics. Among Catholics today the study and devotional reading of Scripture play increasingly important roles in church life.

In contrast to the Roman Catholic view, Luther and other reformers declared that God's will was revealed through Scripture alone. The tradition of the church stood under the authority of the Scriptures, not above them or alongside them. The reformers maintained that the essential teachings of Scripture were clear and they rejected practices of the church that were not grounded in the Bible. Examples of such practices included making financial contributions and pilgrimages to shorten one's time of punishment after death, forbidding priests to marry, and praying to various saints for help. The reformers recognized that the Bible still needed interpretation and they valued the insights of biblical scholars from previous generations, but they insisted that the Scriptures themselves were the touchstone for genuine Christian faith and practice.

The strength of this approach is that the Bible continually challenges people to read and rethink its message. The Scriptures become an ongoing source of reform and renewal in the life of the church. One problem with the emphasis on the Bible as the source of Christian teaching is that Protestants sometimes have perceived the Bible as a collection of truth statements that can be organized into a closed theological system. When this has occurred, renewers of the church have urged people to read the Scriptures for themselves in order to hear its message afresh. Another problem is that the emphasis on "the Bible alone" has prompted some people to reject all traditional interpretations of the Scriptures and formulate their own eccentric understandings of the text.

The book of Revelation provides a useful illustration of these issues. Roman Catholics have been guided in their reading of Revelation by traditional church teachings concerning the end of time. Luther was wary of the book, but concluded that it could be helpful when read in terms of the central message of Scripture, namely the grace of God in Jesus Christ. In the early 1800s, however, a man named John Nelson Darby pieced together select portions of Revelation, Daniel, and other books into his own system of teachings. Darby wanted to show people how to escape the tribulations that would precede the second coming of Christ, which he believed was imminent. The validity of his scheme ultimately depended on peculiar interpretations of a few verses of Scripture. Darby's work has been popularized in the *Scofield Reference Bible* and in *The Late Great Planet Earth* by Hal Lindsey and C. C. Carlson. The Jehovah's Witnesses and other groups have also created systems of teachings about the end times based on their own distinctive collections of passages.

There are several implications that can be drawn from this for people who read the Bible today. First, the community of faith has constantly explored the ways in which the Scriptures continue to be meaningful to people. Some ways of understanding the Bible have stood the test of time, while others have not. We benefit from the insights of other people of faith who read the biblical texts along with us. Second, people sometimes disagree about the contemporary significance of the Bible. Especially when reading difficult passages, it helps to ask what the text might have meant when it was first written before exploring what it might mean for life today. Third, many of the most eccentric interpretations of Scripture are systems based on a few select passages. As you read the Bible, keep the big picture in mind. Ask how a given verse fits into the biblical book you are reading and into the message of the Bible as a whole.

Reading the Bible Today

The world we live in continues to challenge the ways we read and attempt to understand the Bible. Geologists have determined that the earth is billions of years older than the Bible suggests. Paleontologists trace the development of life forms from simple cells all the way to dinosaurs that inhabited a primeval world unknown to the ancient Israelites. Having discovered long ago that the earth is not the center of all things, astronomers continue to probe the reaches of an expanding universe, one not bounded by the gates of heaven. Modern historians, unlike biblical writers, recount the past without reference to miraculous interventions by God, but understand history as the product of interactions among human beings and the world in which they live.

The fruits of modern research have been of tremendous benefit to people. We cannot and should not close our eyes to advances in medical technology, waiting for God to intervene directly in a case of illness. We must make full use of current research into our planet's climate, geological makeup, and the history of its peoples; to neglect these would be irresponsible. At the same time, we must also recognize that there are dimensions of life that transcend the usual categories of technology. When people engaged in scientific research ask questions about the *meaning* of what they see or about the *purpose* of life in this world, they often find themselves asking fundamentally religious questions. How then can the Bible speak meaningfully to people in such a context?

Some people have tried to make the Bible into a modern document by explaining its miracles and other events in terms of natural causes. For example, the biblical text says Jesus fed five thousand people with five loaves and two fish, but some have suggested that everyone had actually brought along enough food, which they shared with others, and that this was the real miracle. Others are content to say that the Bible conveys certain religious truths or provides personal guidance for Christians, but says little about the world or its history. Yet when we read the Bible on its own terms, without attempting to make it fit too quickly into our usual ways of thinking about things, we may find ourselves seeing things in new ways.

After World War II, when the horrors of the systematic destruction of millions of people, especially European Jews, became known, a German theologian was lecturing to a group of college students. During the course of his talk he mentioned the devil several times. Afterward a student politely asked him why he had mentioned the devil, implying that such a notion was irrelevant in a scientific age. The theologian replied that he had spoken of the devil for two reasons. First, because the devil plays an important role in Scripture. Second, "Because I have seen him" (from *Katallagete,* Winter 1981). The Scriptures became the spectacles that brought the world he had experienced into focus.

When you open the pages of the Bible you will find much that is familiar. The people you will encounter share many of the hopes and fears, strengths and failings of people everywhere. You will also find much that is peculiar. But enter into the world of the Bible. Explore it as it is. As you enter its world you may find yourself viewing your own world with new eyes.

7

Why So Many Different Translations?

Anyone who wants to purchase a Bible today is confronted with a bewildering array of choices. The selection of Bibles at a local bookstore will probably include at least half a dozen different translations, some with the Apocrypha and others without it, some with only the biblical text and others with various study helps. Those who attend a Bible study group may find one member reading a passage aloud from the New Revised Standard Version while another tries to follow along in the Good News Bible and someone else scans the New International Version.

The availability of so many different versions can help readers discover the richness of the Scriptures, but it can also be confusing. If three different versions translate the same biblical passage in three different ways, readers may wonder if anyone really knows what it means. A little background on the ways in which translations are made can shed some light on the differences between the various versions, and comments on the characteristics of some of the Bibles in current use can help readers decide which one might be most appropriate for them.

Reasons for New Translations

For several hundred years the translation known as the King James (or Authorized Version) of 1611 was virtually the only one used by English-speaking Protestants; Roman Catholics had the Douay–Rheims Version, completed in 1609–10 and later revised. In the late nineteenth and early twentieth centuries, a few new English translations began to appear. Then, after the Second World War, the pace accelerated dramatically as various church organizations, Bible societies, scholarly groups, publishers, foundations, and individuals began producing new translations of the ancient texts. There were several reasons for this.

A page from the Latin Vulgate Bible. Its translation was supervised by St. Jerome from A.D. 383 to 405.

First, scholars now had much better Greek, Hebrew, and Aramaic manuscripts on which to base translations. The contents of the Bible were first written down between two and three thousand years ago. These texts were copied by hand and circulated among synagogues and churches throughout the ancient world. The originals were lost long ago and translators have had to rely on copies, which sometimes contain mistakes and changes made by those who transcribed the texts over the centuries. The people who produced the King James Version used Greek, Hebrew, and Aramaic texts based on copies made in the eleventh and twelfth centuries. The Douay–Rheims Version was based on the Latin Bible used by the medieval church.

Scholars subsequently discovered copies of the New Testament from the fourth, third, and even second centuries A.D., as well as many later manuscripts. By comparing thousands of these manuscripts they have been able to establish a text of the Greek New Testament that is much more accurate than the one used for older translations. For example, the King James Version of 1 John 5:7 reads, "For there are three that bear record in heaven, the Father, the Word, and the Holy Ghost: and these three are one." More recent translations omit these words since they did not appear in any Greek manuscripts before the Middle Ages and were clearly not part of the original text of 1 John. The Dead Sea scrolls, which were discovered in 1948, included copies of the Hebrew Old Testament that were a thousand years older than those previously available. Readings from these texts are reflected in some recent translations.

Second, scholars know more about biblical languages and cultures than ever before. The Old Testament contains some words and expressions whose meanings are unknown or unclear. Discoveries of ancient documents and inscriptions written in languages related to Hebrew and Aramaic have helped clarify a number of passages. The King James Version, for example, rendered an obscure Hebrew word as "unicorn," referring to a mythical beast that looked like a horse with a single horn protruding from its forehead. Later, some ancient writings were discovered that contained a similar word meaning "wild ox," so that expression is used in all modern translations.

Third, the English language itself has changed over the centuries. To illustrate, let us turn back the clock to 1382, when John Wycliffe published the first complete English translation of the Bible. His version of Matthew 2:16 read, "Thanne Eroude seynge that he was disseyued of the astomyenes, was ful wrooth; and he sent and slowe alle the children that weren in Bethleem. . . ." The language is scarcely intelligible to us anymore. We move ahead in time to 1611, when the King James Version appeared and the verse read, "Then Herod, when he saw that he was mocked of the wise men, was exceeding wroth, and sent forth, and slew all the children that were in Bethlehem. . . ." The language still seems archaic, but at least we can understand it. We move ahead again to 1946, when the Revised Standard Version translated it, "Then Herod saw that he had been tricked by the wise men, was in a furious rage, and he sent and killed all the male children in Bethlehem. . . ." At last we feel like the text is speaking our language.

The English language continues to change. In the 1940s and 50s, many churches used the old words *thou* and *thee* in prayers, and these words continued to appear in the prayers found in most biblical translations. By the 1970s, however, many people preferred to address God as "you," and the words *thou* and *thee* have been dropped from recent translations. Another change has been a desire to avoid using male terminology for groups that include both women and men. Beginning in the 1980s, translators have increasingly referred to "people," the "human race," or even used the old expression "mortals," rather than "men" and "mankind."

Producing a Translation

The people who translate the ancient Hebrew, Aramaic, and Greek texts into modern English are concerned with two things: accuracy and readability. They must accurately translate what the ancient authors wrote, yet do so in a way that reads well in contemporary English. Consider, for example, how Philippians 1:12 sounds if we simply substitute English words for the Greek ones: "To know now you brethren I want that the things to me rather for the advancement of the gospel have come." The sentence is unintelligible in that form and translators must decide how to turn it into a readable English sentence.

The Gospell off S. Luke.

Or as moche as ma=
ny have taken in hond to
compyle a treates off thoo thyns
gf / which are surely knowen a=
monge vs / even as they decla=
red them vnto vs / which from
the begynynge sawe them with
their eyes / and were misters at
the doyng: I determined also /
as sone as I had searched out di=
ligently all thingf from the begynynge / that the
I wolde wryte vnto the / goode Theophilus / th=
at thou myghtest knowe the certente off thoo this
gf / whereof thou arte informed. I

The Fyrst. Chapter.

At the tyme of Herode kynge of iewry / there
was a certayne prest named Zacarias / off
the course of Abie. And his wyfe was of the do=
ughters of Aaron: And her name was Elizabe=
th. Booth were perfect before god / and walked
in all the lawes ãd ordinacions of the lorde that
no mã coulde fynde fawte with them. And they
had no childe / be cause that Elisabeth was bar=
ren / And booth were wele stricken in age.
Hit cam to passe / as he executed the prestes of=
fice / before god as his course cãm (accordinge
to the custome of the prestes office) his lott was
to bren odourf / And went into the tempte of the

A page from William Tyndale's English translation of the Bible. Tyndale, hounded by church and civil authorities, was eventually executed as a heretic in 1536.

Some try to translate the text word for word as much as possible, adjusting the word order and making other changes only as necessary. This approach works quite well for the Philippians passage quoted above. With only a few modifications the sentence reads, "Now I want you to know, brethren, that the things (which have happened) to me have come for the advancement of the gospel" (author's translation).

Others try to translate the text meaning for meaning, rather than word for word. For example, Psalm 16:7 literally says, "I will bless the Lord who counsels me; even at night my kidneys instruct me." Most English speakers would find it peculiar, if not humorous, to think of people being instructed at night by their kidneys. However, we often speak of knowing something "in our hearts." Therefore all English translations render the passage with the word *heart* instead of *kidneys*. "In the night also my heart instructs me" would then preserve the meaning but not the exact words of the Hebrew text. Translators differ, however, over a passage such as Amos 4:6. The New Revised Standard Version translates it word for word as, "I gave you cleanness of teeth in all your cities. . . ." The expression "cleanness of teeth" is a vivid, but perhaps unfamiliar, way of describing hunger. Therefore, Today's English Version translates the meaning, rather than the individual words of the text: "I was the one who brought famine to all your cities."

Concern for theological clarity also affects translations. In John's Gospel, for example, Jesus declares that he will be the source of "living water," referring to the Spirit that would be given to believers. Then the best Greek texts add, "for as yet *there was no Spirit*, because Jesus was not yet glorified" (John 7:39). The passage is potentially confusing, since elsewhere the Gospel indicates that the Spirit already existed. Therefore many translations paraphrase the passage to say, "for as yet *the Spirit had not been given*, because Jesus was not yet glorified."

Theological differences are reflected in the various translations of Isaiah 7:14, a vigorously disputed passage. The Hebrew text contains a word that often refers simply to a "young woman." Therefore the New Revised Standard Version and several others read, "the young woman is with child and shall bear a son, and shall name him Immanuel." Others sharply disagree with this

82

translation, since Isaiah 7:14 is quoted in Greek in Matthew's Gospel, where the word "virgin" is used, and the Isaiah passage provides vital support for belief in the virginal conception of Jesus. Therefore the New International Version and several others read, "The virgin will be with child and will give birth to a son, and will call him Immanuel."

All English translations interpret the meaning of the biblical text to some extent, but some interpret more extensively than others. The New International Version translates John 1:17 word for word as follows: "For the law was given through Moses; grace and truth came through Jesus Christ." Today's English Version, however, adds words for clarity, so that the text reads, "*God* gave the Law through Moses, *but* grace and truth came through Jesus Christ" (italics added). The translators have specified that the Law does come from God, while sharpening the contrast between the Law and Jesus Christ.

The most far-reaching interpretations appear in the Living Bible, which is not a translation from the Hebrew and Greek, but a free English paraphrase. It reads, "For Moses gave us *only* the Law *with its rigid demands and merciless justice, while* Jesus Christ brought *us* loving forgiveness *as well*" (italics added). None of the words in italics are found in the Greek text; they were included to portray the Law in a highly negative light and to contrast it with the loving forgiveness offered by Jesus. In its effort to show readers how passages should be understood, the paraphrase actually rewrites the text.

Recommended Translations

When you select a translation of the Bible for your own use, keep a couple things in mind. (1) Do you want a translation that generally translates the text word for word or one that renders it meaning for meaning? Either type is fine for personal reading, but those who want to study the Bible should use one of the more literal translations. (2) What kind of English style do you read comfortably? Some versions are quite formal, others more simple and conversational. Try reading sample passages in two or three different translations to get a feel for their use of English.

Many translations come in several editions. For example, one publisher may produce two editions of the New International Version of the Bible. One edition contains only the biblical text while the other edition contains the biblical text, introductions to each book of the Bible, explanatory footnotes, and maps. Other publishers offer their own editions, which contain the same text of the New International Version, but with different introductions and footnotes. Most readers find it helpful to use an edition with brief introductions to the books of the Bible and some explanatory footnotes. Those who plan on studying the Bible should use an edition with more extensive notes, maps, and other helps. When you select an edition for your own use, read the Preface and try to identify the special concerns and perspectives of the people who wrote the explanatory notes accompanying the text.

The following are brief descriptions of some of the most significant modern versions of the Bible.

The *New Revised Standard Version* (NRSV), which appeared in 1989, is the authorized revision of the widely used *Revised Standard Version* (RSV). Both translations were made from the original biblical languages, but seek to retain some of the flavor of the King James Version and its later revisions. The work was done by an interdenominational group of scholars under the sponsorship of the National Council of the Churches of Christ in the U.S.A. For the NRSV, the committee adopted the rule of being "as literal as possible, as free as necessary" in its translation. The NRSV paraphrases more freely than the RSV and attempts to avoid using specifically masculine words for groups of people that may have included women. For example, the NRSV uses "brothers and sisters" rather than "brethren" in Romans 1:13, since the Roman congregation presumably included both men and women. The style of the RSV and NRSV is formal, yet readable, making both of them suitable for reading and more detailed biblical study. The Oxford Annotated editions of the RSV and NRSV reflect current trends in biblical scholarship and provide introductions to biblical books, explanatory notes, maps, and other interpretive helps.

The *New International Version* (NIV) is an original translation of the Bible that was completed in 1978. The impetus for the project came from evangelical and Reformed church groups; the translation itself was sponsored by the New York International

Bible Society and produced by scholars from various Protestant denominations. The translators rendered the texts word for word, as much as possible, in a formal English style. The NIV is suitable for general reading and for more detailed Bible study. It is available in many editions which contain introductory materials, footnotes, and indices. The text and various editions of the NIV usually reflect a conservative-evangelical perspective.

Today's English Version (TEV), also known as the *Good News Bible*, was commissioned by the American Bible Society and completed in 1976. The purpose was to produce an accurate, original translation of the Bible in simple, clear, unambiguous English. Sentences were translated meaning for meaning rather than word for word in an effort to make the material as accessible as possible. The translators avoided using unusual or difficult words and structured sentences in a straightforward way. The TEV is reliable and well-suited to younger readers as well as adults, and can profitably be used alongside a more literal translation in Bible studies. Editions of the TEV are available from several publishers; they regularly include introductions to each book, and some footnotes, maps, and indices.

The *Revised English Bible* (REB), which appeared in 1989, is a major revision of the *New English Bible* (NEB). This version was commissioned by the churches of Great Britain and is primarily a product of British scholarship. The translators rendered the original biblical languages into contemporary English on a meaning for meaning, rather than a word for word basis. The REB is more reserved in its use of paraphrase than the earlier NEB, and it attempts to avoid using specifically masculine terminology for groups of people that may have included women. Editions of the REB include the Apocrypha together with the Old and New Testaments. It is suitable for personal reading or for use alongside another translation in Bible study.

The *New American Bible* is the fruit of Roman Catholic biblical scholarship, which has emerged with renewed vigor in recent decades. In response to a request from church leaders, a group of about fifty scholars from the Catholic Biblical Association, including a few Protestants, produced a new translation of the Bible that was based on the Hebrew, Aramaic, and Greek texts, rather than on the Latin version traditionally used by the church.

Texts are sometimes translated word for word and sometimes meaning for meaning into clear, contemporary English. The entire Bible, including the longer list of books in the Roman Catholic canon, became available in 1970. It has since been revised to eliminate specifically masculine terminology for groups of people that may have included women. The NAB is quite useful for reading and Bible study. It is available in various editions, including *The Catholic Study Bible* (Oxford, 1990), which includes extensive introductory material, explanatory footnotes, study helps, and maps.

The *New Jerusalem Bible* (NJB), first published in 1985, and its predecessor the *Jerusalem Bible* (JB), were inspired by French translations of the Bible by Catholic scholars working in Jerusalem. The English version is based on the original Hebrew, Aramaic, and Greek texts, but adopts the general outlook of its French counterpart. The translators render the text on a meaning-for-meaning basis in a dignified English style, but are cautious in their use of paraphrase. The NJB includes all the books in the Roman Catholic canon. The text is well-suited for both reading and study. Doubleday publishes a study edition and a readers' edition, both of which have introductory material, footnotes, study helps, and maps.

Other Translations

The number of Bible translations available continues to multiply. What follows is an alphabetical listing of some of the other translations in current use.

The Amplified Bible, a project of the Lockman Foundation and Zondervan Publishing House, was completed in 1965. Explanatory words and cross references are included in the text of the translation itself. For example, Genesis 1:1 reads, "In the beginning God (prepared, formed, fashioned,) *and* created the heavens and the earth [Heb 11:3]." The additional material is intended to aid interpretation, but often has the effect of making the biblical text less clear and more difficult to read.

The Bible: A New Translation, by James Moffatt, was first issued in 1922. It aimed at translating the text into effective, contemporary British English. The text is somewhat dated now and includes a number of unusual renderings. For example, God is called "the Eternal," rather than "the Lord" or "Yahweh" as in more recent translations.

The Bible in Basic English was produced under the direction of S. H. Hooke, Professor Emeritus of the University of London, and completed in 1982. The group attempted to translate the biblical text from the original languages into simple English idiom. The vocabulary is limited to one thousand common English words. The constraints on vocabulary sometimes make paraphrase necessary, although paraphrase is often used in other cases as well.

The Complete Bible: An American Translation, began with the New Testament translation by Edgar J. Goodspeed in 1923, and later included a translation of the Old Testament by J. M. Powis Smith and several other scholars. It was an important attempt to make the Bible available in ordinary American English, rather than in the more formal literary style used by the other translations available at that time.

The Holy Bible from Ancient Eastern Manuscripts, by George M. Lamsa, is based on the Syriac version of the Bible rather than the original Hebrew and Greek texts. The Bible used by Syrian Orthodox Christians is known as the "Peshitta." It was translated rather freely from the original languages into Syriac in about the fourth century A.D. While Lamsa's translation of the Syriac is of some interest, readers should base their own reading and study on translations based on the original biblical languages.

The Living Bible, as noted earlier, is not a translation from the original biblical languages, but a rather free paraphrase of the Bible that was completed in 1971. Its author is Kenneth Taylor, who based his work on the American Standard Version of 1901 and on other English translations. This paraphrase has enjoyed wide popularity because it is written in an easy-to-read, conversational style that interprets the text as it goes. The Living Bible has helped make the Scriptures accessible to many people, but those looking for a reliable translation in clear, simple English would do better to use Today's English Version.

The *New American Standard Bible* (NASB) was sponsored by the Lockman Foundation, and completed in 1971. The NASB is a revision of the American Standard Version (ASV) of 1901, which was noted for its literal renderings of the Hebrew, Aramaic, and Greek texts. The group that did the revision continued to follow a word-for-word approach to translation, while making the text conform more closely to contemporary English speech. Words such as *thou* and *thee* are retained in prayers found in the Bible.

The New Century Version (NCV) was produced by a group of conservative evangelical translators under the sponsorship of the World Bible Translation Center. It was completed in 1987. The translation is done in a simple style. Paraphrases occur most often in attempts to avoid words that are not common in ordinary spoken English. For example, the Greek equivalent of "repentance" is rendered "change of heart and life."

The New Jewish Publication Society Bible (NJPS), sometimes called the *New Jewish Version*, appeared in three volumes: the Torah, the Prophets, and the Writings. It was completed in 1982 by a leading group of Jewish scholars. The translators attempted to capture the imagery found in the Hebrew Bible while producing a highly readable English version. The text is useful for study, since a given Hebrew word is translated with the same English word as often as possible. There are also valuable footnotes with alternative translations.

The New King James Version (NKJV), sponsored by Thomas Nelson Publishers, is an attempt to update the King James Version without significantly altering its renderings. Words such as *thou*, *thee*, and other archaic expressions have been changed and some of the longer sentences have been broken up. Words not found in the original Hebrew, Aramaic, and Greek texts are placed in italics. Although the editors sometimes noted places where manuscripts preserved different readings, they based their New Testament work on the Greek text published in the sixteenth century, rather than on the evidence of older Greek manuscripts that have been discovered more recently. The complete NKJV became available in 1982.

The New Testament in Modern English, by J. B. Phillips, was completed in 1958 and subsequently revised. Phillips, an English pastor, wanted to produce an English translation that would evoke the same emotions from readers today as the original writings did from readers in the first century. He did not try to render the same Greek word with the same English word in each case, but tried to find words that would have the desired effect in English. His work is useful for general reading of the Bible.

The *New World Translation of the Holy Scriptures* is produced by the Watchtower Bible and Tract Society, the publishing arm of the Jehovah's Witnesses. The translation contains some peculiar renderings that reflect the theology of the group. For example, in most English versions of the Bible, John 1:1 is regularly and correctly translated, "the Word was God." The *New World Translation*, however, has "the Word was a god," in an attempt to avoid ascribing divinity to Jesus. This translation is used almost exclusively by the Jehovah's Witnesses themselves.

In addition to the many translations noted above, one edition of the Bible needs special comment. In 1909 Cyrus Scofield produced *The Scofield Reference Bible*, which included extensive introductions and comments to the King James Version of the Bible. His notes were revised in 1917 and again in 1967, and are still published in some editions of the King James Version and other translations. The contents of these explanatory notes comprise a system known as "dispensationalism," which tries to detect the exact sequence of events that will happen at the end of time. The footnotes give excessive attention to Daniel, Revelation, and other biblical books. The system was formulated by John Nelson Darby in the early 1800s. More information about his work is found in chapter 6 above.

The sheer number of translations and paraphrases available today can be confusing. Use care in selecting a version and a particular edition of that version. Become familiar with one primary translation. You will find it helpful to consult other versions, especially when you find a difficult passage or are engaged in Bible study, but use one translation as your basic text. In that way the different translations available today can help rather than hinder your reading of the Bible.

8

How Should I Read the Bible?

So far in this book we have surveyed the contents of the Bible and the way in which it was formed. We have noted some of the ways people have understood its message and discussed the characteristics of various translations. What remains to be done is to make some suggestions to guide you when you actually pick up the Bible and begin to read it.

A Plan for Reading the Bible

Begin reading the parts of the Bible that seem most interesting or important to you. You need not begin with Genesis and read each book in sequence. Recall that in chapter 2 we surveyed the many different kinds of material in the biblical library; use that survey to help you identify the books you would like to read first. Many editions of the Bible have introductions to individual books (see also *A Beginner's Guide to the Books of the Bible*, described on p. 98 of this book). These can also help guide your reading.

If you are still uncertain about where to begin, the following sequence might be useful. Read through the Gospels of Mark and John to become more familiar with the story of Jesus' life, death, and resurrection. These Gospels portray Jesus in different ways that can help readers expand their understanding of who Jesus is. Then read the book of Acts, in order to get a better idea of the way the gospel message spread and early Christian communities were formed. Finally, read one or more of Paul's letters, which address the concerns of these early communities. Paul's letter to the Philippians is short, warm, and personal, offering an intense and moving glimpse into the heart of the Christian faith. His letter to the Romans is longer, presenting a summary of Paul's preaching.

When you turn to the Old Testament, you may find it helpful to begin by reading all of Genesis and the first twenty chapters of Exodus. These chapters take readers from the creation to the pivotal events of Israel's escape from Egypt and the giving of the commandments on Mt. Sinai. Then turn to the book of Psalms, which contains some of the Bible's best-loved hymns and prayers. The book of Psalms is quite long, but read at least the first section (Psalms 1–41), which contains a good selection of Psalms, including prayers for help, exuberant hymns, prayers of thanksgiving, and contemplative writings. Finally, become acquainted with one of the books of the prophets. The book of Micah is short and written in the poetic style typical of the prophetic books; it contains messages of warning and hope. Isaiah and Jeremiah are much longer. Isaiah is written almost entirely in poetry and is more widely read among Christians; Jeremiah contains both poetic passages and narratives about the prophet's life.

This selection of Old and New Testament books will acquaint you with the main types of material found in the Bible. Continue by reading in the areas that seem most interesting to you. Important books to consider include the other Gospels, the remaining letters of Paul, and 1 Peter in the New Testament. In the Old Testament, you may find it helpful to read the chapters recounting Israel's journey to the promised land (Exodus 32–34; Numbers 11–17 and 20–25), and the stories of the conquest and kingdom found in Joshua through 2 Kings. The events recounted in 2 Kings 18–25 provide the context for the work of some of Israel's prophets. If you have not read Isaiah and Jeremiah already, read them after 2 Kings. Many people find it meaningful to read one or two Psalms each day, using them as a basis for prayer or personal reflection.

Understanding What You Read

When you first read through a portion of the Bible, avoid getting entangled in difficult passages. If some parts of the Bible seem confusing, just keep reading; you can return to them later. Especially at first it is important to gain a feel for the material and a sense of the whole. Often it can be helpful to read through an entire book of the Bible twice. Some people read a book quickly, then go back over it more slowly; others read it carefully first, then page through it a second time to gain a clearer sense of the whole.

Recall that some books in the Bible are collections of materials from various sources rather than unified compositions by a single author. We noted that in Genesis 6:19-22, for example, God commanded Noah to bring one pair of each species of animals into the ark, but in 7:1-5 he commanded Noah to bring in seven pairs of each species. Two accounts of the story have apparently been combined into a single narrative. The differences in detail can be puzzling, but the flow of the story as a whole is clear. We also noted that the prophetic books contain messages that were originally delivered at various times and places. The section headings and footnotes included in many Bibles can help you follow the sequence of material.

Some parts of the Bible include long genealogies, prescriptions for sacrifices, census figures, and other technical materials. Don't get bogged down in these sections. Skim over them at first; try to keep the main line of the story in mind. Most Bibles have headings at the top of each page to help you identify where you are in the narrative; some Bibles also have footnotes with additional helps for understanding the text. Use the headings and footnotes to help you keep your bearings as you read.

Remember that you already have many of the skills essential for reading the Bible. Like a newspaper, the Bible contains different kinds of material. Within its pages you will find poetry, history, prophecy, proverbs, parables, and much more. The reading skills you already have will help you approach each kind of material in an appropriate way.

When you read the Bible carefully, you will have questions about it. Identify the questions you think are most important and pursue them. Some questions can be answered by locating additional information. For example, you may wonder when or where an event took place, or be puzzled by a biblical custom. A Bible dictionary or the footnotes in a good study Bible can often help clarify such matters. Other questions deal with broad issues of meaning, such as "Why did Jesus die?" A Bible dictionary may be of some help here, but you will probably want to ask a pastor for additional counsel as you think about these issues. Many questions have no neat and simple answer, but you may discover that some ways of thinking about a problem are more constructive than others.

You may wish to look at *A Beginner's Guide to Studying the Bible,* described on p. 98 of this book. It gives basic helps for studying short passages, chapters, or whole books of the Bible, and also tells how to use resource books such as commentaries, concordances, Bible dictionaries, and atlases.

Reading the Bible Devotionally

Read some books of the Bible again and again, until you become very familiar with them. Once you have a sense for the breadth of material in the Bible, read several of the books in depth, letting them become your own. For example, read one gospel again and again and ponder its message. Return to it often until you know its story well. Use a pencil to underline verses that are especially meaningful. Read these verses aloud, then commit them to memory as a resource to draw on wherever you may be.

Passages from the Bible can help Christians put their prayers into words. The most difficult moment of a prayer may be the first moment, as people try to focus the thoughts they want to bring before God. Passages from the Psalms and other parts of the Bible provide us with words to express the joy, sadness, anger, and hope that we feel. For example, Psalm 121 begins, "I lift up my eyes to the hills—from where will my help come? My help comes from the LORD, who made heaven and earth." By beginning a prayer with words like these, we may find it easier to give voice to our own needs and concerns later in the prayer.

Another way the Bible helps us pray is by telling the stories of others who have turned to Christ for help. John 4:46-54, for example, recounts how an official went to Jesus when his son was seriously ill and how Jesus healed the boy. We may begin a prayer by remembering how Jesus responded to that need, then continue by asking God to restore the health of someone we know.

Some people find it helpful to read the Bible along with a devotional booklet. These booklets usually have people read a passage from the Bible, then offer a brief reflection on the meaning of the passage for life today. Others find it more meaningful to write down their thoughts about the Bible passages they read. One way to do this is to read a chapter from the Bible, then summarize it in a sentence or two. As people write these summaries they think about the central message of the chapter. Keeping a journal of such reflections can help you uncover the meaning of the Scriptures.

The books of the Bible were written down centuries ago in a world that differs from ours in many ways. Some passages speak easily across the centuries; others seem peculiar or irrelevant to our time. But keep in mind that the Scriptures were first written down in ways that addressed the needs of the community of faith; they were preserved because they continued to speak to issues confronting people in subsequent generations. Let the Bible speak in its own way; enter into its world; ask what it might have said to the men and women who first read it or heard it. As you do so, you may find yourself viewing your own world in a new way.

Reading the Bible with Others

The Bible can be a very personal book, unmatched in its ability to speak to the experiences and questions of individuals. But if the Bible can be personal, it is certainly not private. The Bible can be read in moments of solitude, but should also be read with other people. The books of the Bible were intended to be read by whole communities of faith. Paul sent his letters to the congregations at Rome, Corinth, and other places. When the letters arrived, they were read aloud to those who gathered for worship. In the Old Testament, the people of Israel were told to keep the Lord's commandments in their hearts and to "recite them to your children and talk about them when you are at home and when you are away" (Deuteronomy 6:6-7).

The same is true for Christians today. Worship services regularly include several Bible readings and a sermon based on a biblical text. Most congregations also offer opportunities to study the Bible along with others. Bible study groups usually devote part of each session to looking at the message of a particular biblical text, allowing some time to explore how that text may speak to Christians today. Some Bible study groups meet weekly throughout the year. Other groups may agree simply to meet for four or six weeks in order to study a particular book, without expecting participants to make a longer time commitment.

A structured Bible study group is a good way to grow with the Bible, but it is not the only way. Reading the Bible with others can become part of the rhythm of the day. Some people make a commitment with a spouse or a friend to read the same Bible passages and then talk about them over coffee or lunch. Reading Bible stories with children also can be very rewarding. Bible story books vary considerably in the quality of their artwork and the vocabulary level used in the text. Select a book suitable for the ages of your children. Bible stories often prompt children to ask interesting questions (including some that may not have occurred to you) that can help all of you grow in your understanding of the text. Those who read and study the Bible together with others usually learn more than they could on their own, because people help each other to see new things and to explore the connections between biblical texts and daily life.

The world within the Bible awaits you. When you open the Scriptures and begin to read, you will embark on a journey of discovery. The journey is open-ended; each time you traverse the Bible's pages you may find new insights even in familiar texts. You will not travel alone. Many have gone before you, many will follow; and the Spirit of God will accompany you on the way. Each journey has to have a starting point; why not choose one and begin?

For Further Reading

Recommended Bibles

The Holy Bible. New Revised Standard Version. Augsburg Fortress gift and award edition. Minneapolis: Augsburg Fortress, 1990. Includes an introduction to the books of the Bible, study helps, a modest dictionary-concordance, and color maps.

The New Oxford Annotated Bible. New Revised Standard Version. New York: Oxford University Press, 1991. Includes introductions to each book of the Bible, informative footnotes, maps, and interpretive essays on various approaches to biblical study, the kinds of material contained in the Bible, and a survey of the geography, history, and archaeology of the Bible lands.

The New Oxford Annotated Bible with the Apocrypha. New York: Oxford University Press, 1991. Same as above entry, except that this edition includes the intertestamental books accepted as part of the Bible by Roman Catholic and Eastern Orthodox Christians.

Good News Bible: The Bible in Today's English Version. American Bible Society. Published by various publishers. An easy-to-read but reasonably accurate translation for those looking for ease of understanding. Includes an index, cross references, a word list, and maps.

Concordance

NRSV Exhaustive Concordance. Edited by Bruce M. Metzger. Nashville: Thomas Nelson, 1991. Indexes all occurrences of most words in the New Revised Standard Version of the Bible.

Bible Dictionary

Harper's Bible Dictionary. Edited by Paul Achtemeier. San Francisco: Harper & Row, 1985. Contains 3700 articles by leading biblical scholars on the books, places, people, and major ideas in the Bible, as well as outlines of all the books of the Bible. Includes color maps and photos.

Bible Commentary

Harper's Bible Commentary. Edited by James L. Mays. San Francisco: Harper & Row, 1988. This fully illustrated and reliable one-volume commentary includes introductions and explanatory notes for each book of the Old and New Testaments and the Apocrypha. The contributors are an interdenominational group of leading biblical scholars.

Geography of the Bible

Basic Biblical Geography. By Denis Baly. Minneapolis: Fortress Press, 1987. A concise overview of the geography of Palestine and the Transjordan.

Other Bible Helps and Resources

A Beginner's Guide to the Books of the Bible. By Diane L. Jacobson and Robert Kysar. Minneapolis: Augsburg, 1991. Gives concise, easy-to-understand introductions to each of the 39 books of the Old Testament and the 27 books of the New Testament.
A Beginner's Guide to Studying the Bible. By Rolf E. Aaseng. Minneapolis: Augsburg, 1991. Provides basic steps for studying shorter passages or whole books of the Bible. Describes helpful resources such as concordances, atlases, and Bible dictionaries.
The Joy of Discovery in Bible Study. By Oletta Wald. Minneapolis: Augsburg, 1975. Teaches six study skills for a better understanding of the Bible and finding meaning for daily life.

Maps

MAP 1

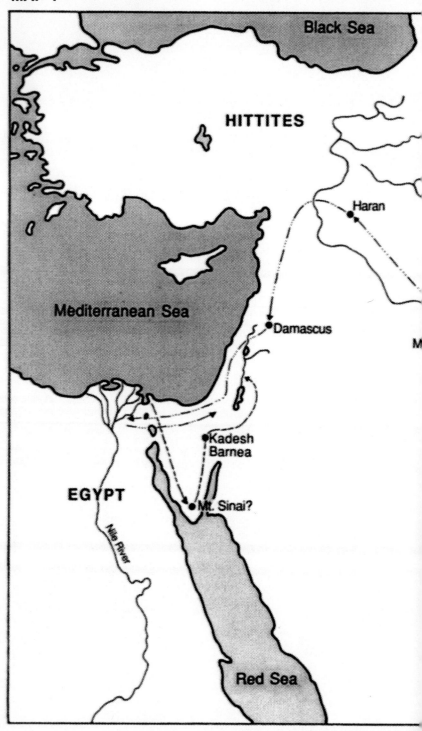

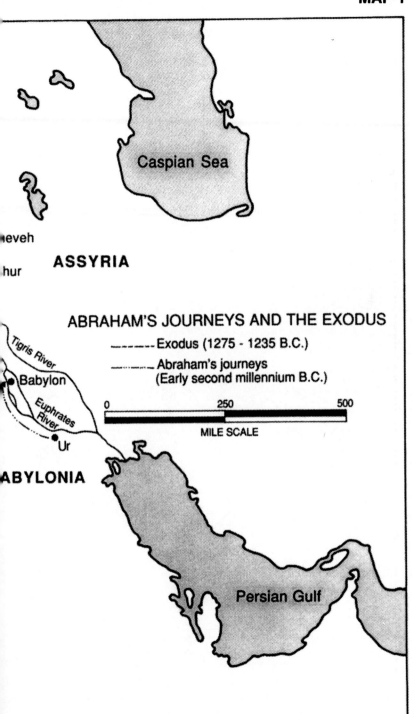

MAP 1

ABRAHAM'S JOURNEYS AND THE EXODUS

------- Exodus (1275 - 1235 B.C.)

_____ Abraham's journeys
(Early second millennium B.C.)

MILE SCALE

MAP 2

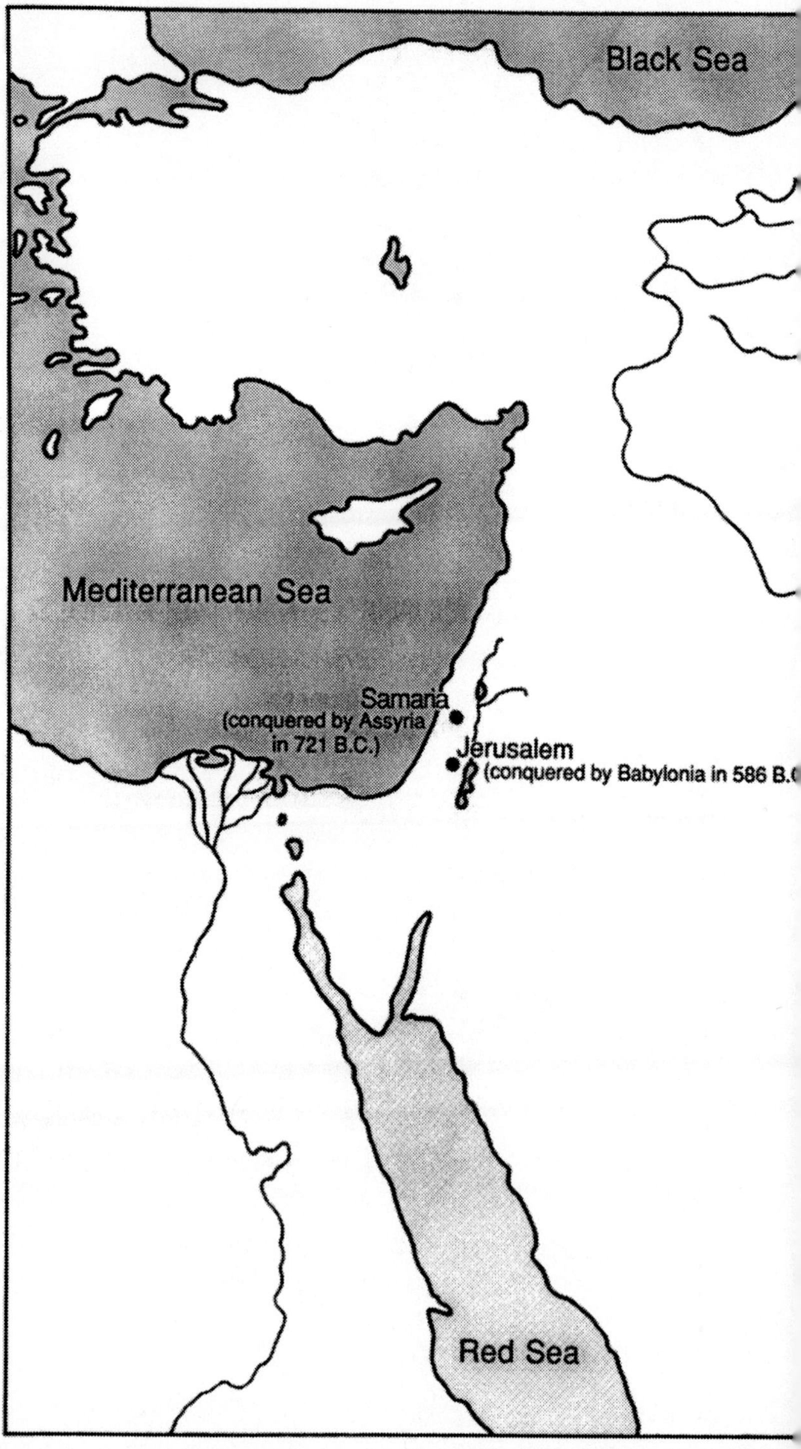

Black Sea

Mediterranean Sea

Samaria
(conquered by Assyria
in 721 B.C.)

Jerusalem
(conquered by Babylonia in 586 B.C.

Red Sea

MAP 2

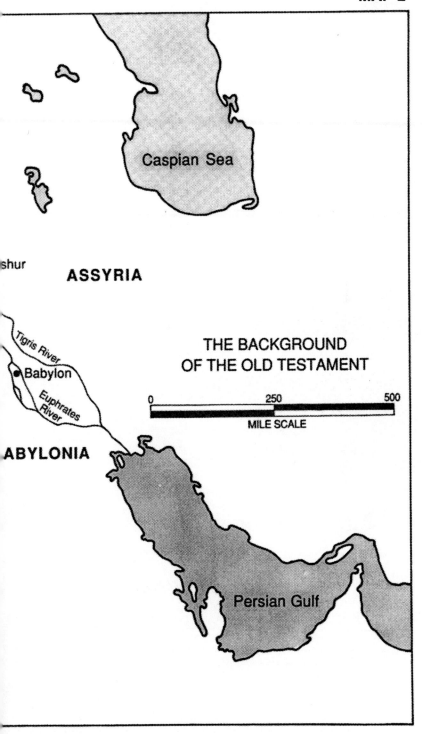

shur

ASSYRIA

Caspian Sea

Tigris River

●Babylon

Euphrates River

**THE BACKGROUND
OF THE OLD TESTAMENT**

0   250   500

MILE SCALE

ABYLONIA

Persian Gulf

MAP 3

Sidon

Damascus

PHOENICIA

ARAM

Tyre

The Great Sea

Samaria

ISRAEL

AMMON

Rabbah

Jerusalem

PHILISTIA

JUDAH

Gaza

MOAB

THE KINGDOMS OF
ISRAEL AND JUDAH

---- Approximate boundaries
of Israel and Judah

Kir-hareseth

0   25   50

MILE SCALE

EDOM

MAP 4

Mediterranean Sea

PHOENICIA

Sidon

Tyre

Damascus

SYRIA

Caesarea Philippi

Capernaum

Sea of
Galilee

GALILEE

Nazareth

Caesarea

Sebaste
(Samaria)

SAMARIA

Jordan River

DECAPOLIS

PEREA

JUDEA

Jericho

Jerusalem

Bethlehem

Dead
Sea

Masada

IDUMEA

PALESTINE IN
NEW TESTAMENT TIMES

0   25   50

MILE SCALE

MAP 5

MACEDONIA

Philip

Thessalonica

Berea

ACHAIA

Corinth

Athe

ITALIA

Rome

SICILIA

MALTA

Mediterranean Sea

CRE

CYRENE

THE BACKGROUND OF THE NEW TESTAMENT

☐ Places to which Paul's letters were addressed

0   250   500

MILE SCALE

MAP 5

Black Sea

s(Alexandria)

GALATIA □

ASIA

Ephesus

Colossae

Tarsus

Antioch

CYPRUS

SYRIA

Damascus

Mediterranean Sea

Caesarea

Jerusalem

ARABIA

EGYPT

Red Sea

MAP 6

Black Sea

Ankara

TURKEY

CYPRUS
Nicosia

Mediterranean Sea

LEBANON
Bayrut (Beirut)

SYRIA

Dimashq
(Damascus)

IR

ISRAEL
Jerusalem

Amman

JORDAN

El Qahira
(Cairo)

Nile River

SAUDI ARABI

EGYPT

Red Sea

SUDAN

MAP 6

VIET UNION

SOVIET UNION

Caspian Sea

•Tehran

IRAN

Baghdad

THE MIDDLE EAST TODAY

Euphrates River

0   250   500

MILE SCALE

KUWAIT •Al Kuwayt

Persian Gulf

BAHRAIN
Al Manamah

QATAR
Ad Dawhah

•Ar Riyad

Abu Dhabi•

UNITED ARAB
EMIRATES   OMAN

CPSIA information can be obtained at www.ICGtesting.com
Printed in the USA
LVOW08s0918080114

368476LV00001B/26/A

9 780806 625706